D0105568

796.426 Ber
Beresini, Erin
Off course : inside the
   mad, muddy world of
   obstacle course racing
                          $25.00
               ocn867078132
               10/28/2014

OFF COURSE

OFF COURSE

///

INSIDE THE MAD, MUDDY WORLD
OF OBSTACLE COURSE RACING

Erin Beresini

Houghton Mifflin Harcourt

BOSTON · NEW YORK

2014

Copyright © 2014 by Erin Beresini

All rights reserved

For information about permission to reproduce selections from this book,
write to Permissions, Houghton Mifflin Harcourt Publishing Company,
215 Park Avenue South, New York, New York 10003.

www.hmhco.com

This book presents the ideas of its author. You should consult with a
professional health care provider before commencing any exercise plan.
The author and the publisher disclaim liability for any adverse effects
resulting directly or indirectly from information contained herein.

Library of Congress Cataloging-in-Publication Data
Beresini, Erin.
Off course : inside the mad, muddy world of obstacle
course racing / Erin Beresini.
pages cm
ISBN 978-0-544-05532-2 (hardcover)
1. Obstacle racing. I. Title.
GV1067.B47 2014
796.42'6 — dc23
2014016523

Book design by Chrissy Kurpeski

Printed in the United States of America
DOC 10 9 8 7 6 5 4 3 2 1

The epigraph is taken from *What Matters Most Is How You Walk Through
the Fire* by Charles Bukowski. Copyright © by Linda Lee Bukowski.
Reprinted by permission of HarperCollins Publishers.

Spartan Race Beast course map courtesy of Spartan Race Inc./
Mapping Specialists, Ltd.

For Jimmy,
for putting up with me

And for my parents,
ditto, and for their love and support

And for Jimmy again,
double ditto

Spartan Race Beast

KILLINGTON, VERMONT

SEPTEMBER 22–23

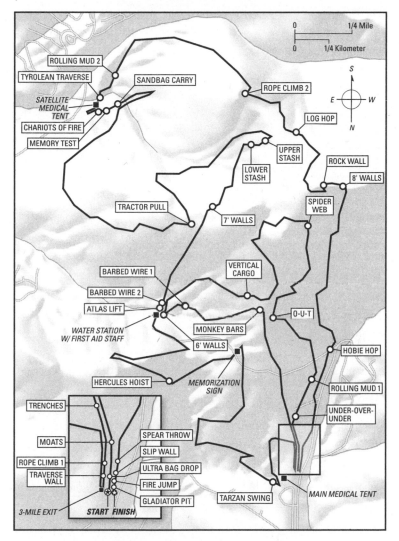

Multiply by two for the Ultra Beast

what matters most is
how well you
walk through the
fire.

— CHARLES BUKOWSKI

Contents

OFF COURSE

1

If It's Broke

I'M FACE-DOWN IN the mud. Sharp rocks are poking into my forearms, stomach, and thighs. I'm pretty sure I just lost a big tuft of hair to the barbed wire zigzagged inches above my head, and I don't want to move because a sadistic man with an enormous hose will blast me again with arctic water if he thinks I'm advancing too fast. "You don't roll in the Marines! You'll get shot!" somebody barked at me moments ago. Then came the first icy spray.

Stay dry. That's the only way I'll survive out here in the cool autumn forest. Get wet, and hypothermia could set in fast. I'm already shivering, but I'm not soaked.

I've got at least thirty more feet of barbed wire to pass under before I can stand again, so right now I have a decision to make: roll forward and plunge into a chilly puddle, or crawl sideways where the ground is more mud than water and risk entering prime hose-blast range.

Those are not your standard Saturday morning choices. Oatmeal or pancakes? To get up or not to get up? That's more like it. What I would do for a down comforter and a Tetley tea right now.

"Keep going!" someone inching up behind me says. Less than one hour and three miles after this torture began, it looks like we're both about to get drenched. Even worse, we have twenty-four miles to go, and this suffering is nothing compared to what's coming next.

REDONDO BEACH, CALIFORNIA
SIX MONTHS EARLIER

I was a broken athlete. Physically, mentally, and spiritually, I had nothing left. I'd spent eight months in a melancholy funk, wondering when and how I would get my health and motivation back. And like most spectacular breakdowns, this one had been a long time coming.

I had raced my first triathlon in Tucson in 2005, and I sucked at it. The run was only three miles long but felt like thirty, and it nearly triggered a finish-line upchuck. But the mediocrity I displayed that day sparked something inside of me. I looked at my magnificently fit competitors whose muscles bulged through their spandex and decided I wanted to be like them. Not just like them — I wanted to beat them. I knew I could do better if I tried. And since I was about to graduate from college with a degree in French, I didn't have a lot to look forward to career-wise.

After graduation, I moved to Los Angeles with visions of becoming a screenwriter—or maybe an advertising copywriter—and I started racing more triathlons. I learned to accept spandex as a valid category of apparel and found out the hard way why bike shorts are meant to be worn without underwear. I spent a lot of time at my local triathlon shop questioning the sales guy, Robert, about time trial bikes, aero bars, and neon foods that are neither liquid nor solid.

Perhaps to get me out of his hair, Robert took it upon himself to introduce me to other people, usually at the most inopportune times. Like at an Olympic distance triathlon in Ventura. I had just completed the race and was covered in my own sweat and snot. I still didn't feel comfortable wearing spandex in public—it did nothing to enhance my figure, which was somewhat swollen from the stress of adulthood. Salt rings had formed in strange places on my tank top and shorts, emphasizing my jiggly bits. I was about to change clothes when Robert walked up to me with an incredibly hot male triathlete by his side.

"Erin!" Robert said. "I want you to meet someone."

Oh God. I struck an awkward pose in an attempt to simultaneously cover up my tummy chub and elongate my legs.

"Jimmy, this is Erin. She also got second in your age group."

That was it. That was all Robert had to say. Then he just stood there like he'd lit a bottle rocket and was waiting for the fuse to burn down.

"Congratulations," Jimmy said.

"You too," I said.

When my car broke down a month later, I asked Jimmy for a ride to a race we were both doing in Flagstaff, Arizona.

On the drive home, I called my mom to tell her I was going to marry Jimmy. He was fun, fit, fast, kind, and a little weird, and I loved him. He proposed seven months later.

Since Robert was clearly gifted at setting me up with like-minded people, even if his timing was a little off, I was excited when he introduced me to a group of athletes who were training to race Ironman Arizona. I didn't know what an Ironman was, but I wanted in. I'd spent about half a year in Los Angeles and still couldn't call myself anything other than an hourly-wage product description writer who worked in a freezing cold warehouse and lived off of the old, hard gumballs I'd found in a box under my desk. I desperately wanted to call myself an Ironman and give my parents something to brag about to their friends. *Oh, your Jennifer went to Harvard Law and is now a partner at a prestigious New York law firm? Well, my daughter is an Ironman.*

So, in April 2007, after twelve hours and one minute of swimming, biking, and running, I became an Ironman. I was elated to cross the finish line, but then I started wondering how much better I could do if I tried harder. And so began the cycle of training for and racing in endurance events, each a little bigger and a little badder than the next. Training became a way of life—and the way I continued to meet new friends as an adult.

When I went back to school to get a degree in the more useful but vaguely named field of "communications," I joined the university's triathlon team. Instant friends. While I interned after graduating, I competed in another Ironman and a 100-mile mountain bike race. Instant respect. By the time I landed my dream job at a San Diego fitness rag, there was only one thing left to do: Ultraman, a three-day, 320-mile triathlon.

"You do realize it'll probably take you months to recover

from this," Jimmy warned when I called to tell him that I was
going to sign up for Ultraman Canada. Jimmy was still working in Los Angeles, and we were living apart on weekdays. Ultraman training would help fill the void created by Jimmy's
absence and prevent me from replacing him with chocolate
cake. It would also be my revenge on Race Across Oregon, a
516-mile cycling race that was the only event I'd ever quit.

It happened in July 2009. I had been riding my bike 376
miles straight into a headwind when something in my brain
broke.

Why the hell are you doing this? a unicorn walking alongside
of me asked.

I don't know, I replied. *Why are you talking to me?*

Offended, my hallucination trotted into the trees while I
climbed into the minivan with my crew for a break and never
got back out. I'd felt guilty about quitting ever since. Ultraman would fix that.

The endurance gods smiled upon me during training, and
I never once got injured. I did get pulled off of the Los Angeles Marathon course at mile 24 with hypothermia—it was
windy, rainy, and in the 50s—but the gods made up for it two
months later when they let me qualify for the Boston Marathon. Life as an athlete was peachy. Life by the border without
Jimmy, however, was sad.

When it became clear he couldn't move south anytime
soon, I had a heart-to-heart with my boss. Working remotely
was not an option, she said. Sometimes you have to choose
between your career and your family.

So I had a heart-to-heart with my landlord. "Honey, every
day you get with your husband is a blessing. Go to him!" she
said. For the low, low price of an extra month's rent, Park
Place Apartments would release me to my man.

I left San Diego about a month before Ultraman, so I had plenty of time to burn a swim-cap tan into my forehead while training at noon in LA's outdoor pools.

Ultraman itself was magical. It was fun to compete without having to think about a thing because my crew had it all covered. Jimmy kayaked alongside me, guiding me 6.2 miles across Skaha Lake, handing me GUs every half-hour, and wondering why I couldn't pee and swim at the same time. Justin, a former tri teammate, dangled PB&Js and Gatorade and potato chips so I could grab them as I whizzed by on my bike. And when my stomach acted up on the double marathon, my father-in-law, Steve, held up a towel so I could relieve myself on the side of the road, my own personal porta-potty.

When my crew realized I was actually going to finish the event, they were overjoyed. I was overjoyed. Together we ran the last half-mile down the road, into a grassy park, and across the finish line.

I uploaded a new Facebook cover photo. In it, I'm wearing a Wonder Woman bathing suit with a towel cape and running out of Skaha Lake with a triumphant fist in the air. I look like a superhero. I felt like a superhero. At that moment there was absolutely nothing I couldn't do.

I never imagined that only one month later I'd be sitting across from my doctor as he reviewed dozens of blood tests, trying to figure out what had gone so horribly wrong.

It's diabetes, I thought as I sat in Dr. W's office looking at his Ironman Arizona finisher photo on the wall. He had beaten my best time by ten minutes. I would have to do something about that, but not right now. I was in his office because I couldn't move.

Spontaneous diabeticus, my unmedical definition of adult-onset type 1 diabetes, seemed like the only logical diagnosis. My dad got it when he was forty-three, just months after completing the Big Sur Marathon. Mom thought the event weakened his immune system, letting a virus destroy his pancreas. I've had pancreatic paranoia ever since.

In my favor, I wasn't thirsty or peeing all of the time. And I certainly hadn't lost any weight. I was just tired. So tired that I couldn't get out of bed some days. My cat, Sir Galahad, was an eager companion, but he didn't quite have the wit or the amusing stories of my former cubemate. Instead, he developed the annoying habit of eating my yogurt at the same time I did and typing indecipherable statements in the middle of my stories, like: lkjargjklaegrere31.

Worst of all, I couldn't do what I'd always done whenever I felt down: go for a run, or a bike ride, or a swim. My body was broken. I'd jog down the beach and feel like I had to sleep after ten minutes of movement. I pictured myself passing out in the sand only to wake up hours later when some old man poked me with his metal detector.

Years ago Dr. W had likened me to a Ferrari because my heart hiccups at low speeds but runs famously at high speeds. I was meant for endurance sports, it seemed. But now Dr. W had another analogy all whipped up for me. This time I wasn't a Ferrari—I was a drug addict.

"Your blood looks fantastic," he said first.

"Great," I said. I wasn't diabetic. "So why am I so tired?"

"Let's look at it this way," Dr. W explained. "If I were going to take one of my patients off of antidepressants, I'd never just pull the plug. I'd gradually bring the dose down."

"Okay."

"Your Ultraman training was like an antidepressant," he continued. "You gradually upped your training until you were working out more than twenty hours a week. Your body got used to having a high dose of endorphins."

"So this is all an endorphin crash?"

"Well—"

"Overtraining syndrome?"

"Well, let's look at what overtraining syndrome is," he said. "It's physical and mental. Are you tired because you're sad? Or are you sad because you're tired? It's hard to tell."

I pulled the bill of my hat down lower to avoid eye contact with him. I thought I'd cry. Or barf. I had almost hoped there was something physically wrong with me so I could take a magic pill and be done with it. Now he was telling me it was all in my head.

Dr. W concluded the visit by handing me the card of a "wonderful, down-to-earth" psychiatrist in Manhattan Beach who was "not at all weird."

I chucked the card and spent the rest of the year in hibernation, freelancing from home and dragging myself to my neighbor's house a few times a week to slog through Insanity workout videos. While she contemplated Shawn T.'s age and whether or not his abs were spray-painted on, I wondered when I'd feel normal again.

I spent Thanksgiving and Christmas sleeping in my childhood bedroom in Phoenix instead of running with my dad as usual.

Finally, in January, I started to feel better. Not great, but better. I started running again to get in shape for the Boston Marathon and decided I should do the American Birkebeiner cross-country ski race in Wisconsin in February. I'd never cross-country-skied before, and that's precisely why it seemed like a great idea—I needed to try something new. Mix it up a little and give my brain a break.

And that's how I landed myself back in Dr. W's office again for the second time since Ultraman.

"Let me get this straight," Dr. W said as he squeezed my hairy ankles. "You went to do a thirty-four-mile cross-country ski race without having skied before?"

"Well, I intended to practice," I said. "But it never snowed anywhere near LA this year."

I had Achilles tendonitis, and I had it bad. Jimmy sawed off the back halves of my old running shoes just so I could put them on. The slightest pressure on the outside of my heels felt like someone lit a campfire between my tendons and my bones.

Dr. W told me to sleep with boots on to keep my Achilles from tightening up and to lay off running for a while, effectively halting my sex life and my metabolism in one sentence.

A month later I tried to run again. I had to. Boston was coming up, and I wasn't sure I'd ever have it in me to qualify again, so I went for a flat, five-mile training run. Then something in my right calf swelled up.

"The good news," Dr. W said while he squeezed my hairy calf, "is that your Achilles is still attached."

"Will I rupture it if I run Boston?" I asked.

"Probably not," he said. "If you want to run, run. But pay attention to yourself, and know that it's definitely going to set back your healing."

I quit running altogether, but still had every intention of

doing Boston. Then, just five days before the race, I got a fever. My head and chest filled with phlegm. I couldn't get out
of bed.

"The good news is you don't have the flu." This time it was
Dr. Tong speaking through a medical face mask. Dr. W didn't
have any last-minute appointments, or maybe he was just sick
of seeing me and my furry limbs. Dr. Tong gave me a Z-Pak
and an inhaler and sent me home with Jimmy.

When our plane touched down at Logan International
Airport the next day, I got an email from the Boston Athletic
Association that saved me from complete and total self-de-
struction and served as a virtual sign that I'd hit rock bottom.

"The weather situation continues to be a significant concern for Boston Marathoners," it read, referring to the 88-de-
gree weather forecast for marathon day. "We strongly rec-
ommend that . . . you accept the deferment option from the
B.A.A. . . . Again, if you have any medical problems or if you
are under-trained, then please do not run this marathon."

It was like the BAA was speaking directly to me. I had to
fly all the way to Boston and get this email to finally realize
that my body was done with long, solitary endurance efforts.
My brain didn't want to focus on that stuff anymore. It was
so bored with that type of workout that it shut me down for
months to try to get me to do something else, but I didn't listen. So it filled itself with phlegm and started blowing snot
bubbles out of my nose to avoid having to run another marathon. Now I was listening.

But I'm an Ironman, I thought. *That's what I do.*

There was only one person I could speak to who would
understand my existential endurance predicament.

· · ·

Robyn Dunn is my athletic twin. She's also blond, an Iron-man, and an ultracyclist. We had shared our first Ironman, our first double-century bike ride, and our first years living in Los Angeles. We'd huddled for hours in a ditch on the side of the road when we got caught in sleet on a bike ride, and we'd confronted snakes on trail runs. She's also exactly five years older than I am, which is ideal in any endurance friend-ship, because we will never be in the same age group. We can compete as hard as we want, and if we both do well, we both win.

Robyn was equally dedicated to pushing herself harder, faster, and longer than she'd ever thought possible, and she was becoming a true force to be reckoned with on the South-ern California trail-running circuit. In fact, she was running a grueling 50K at the mountainous Malibu Creek State Park when everything went bad for her. She felt like she couldn't breathe, like her lungs were on fire. They hurt so much that she couldn't finish the race, and Robyn never quits. Some-thing was terribly wrong.

A few days later I took her to the hospital.

"I have blood clots in my lungs," she cried when her CT results came back.

I couldn't believe it. She'd run almost thirty-one miles a few days earlier, and now doctors were telling her that she'd have to be on blood thinners for a year. She couldn't ride a bike. Trail running wasn't advisable. She couldn't drink alcohol. Ba-sically, she wasn't supposed to do anything that might bruise her, because it would put her at risk for internal bleeding.

It was impossible to imagine what Robyn was going through. In an instant, her athletic identity was snatched away for an entire year. Sure, there were tears and frustration—and maybe a few self-pity beers—but Robyn stayed positive and focused on the things she could do. She took spin classes and joined a beach volleyball club. She ran on the sidewalk. By the end of the year, she had serious volleyball skills, a greater aerobic engine than she'd had to start, and dozens of new friends. She even had a new boyfriend, a runner named Albert. She persevered and came out of the experience a better, stronger athlete and a happier person.

And so I sought Robyn's counsel now. I knew she'd understand how I felt about realizing I needed a break from being an Ironman.

Robyn had three words for me: obstacle course racing. Clearly, she hadn't done it during her year on blood thinners, but it was a new passion she and Albert had discovered. The training was different, she said. More power and agility exercises, fewer long, mind-numbing miles. And the events were truly a challenge.

Robyn and Albert had recently run a "Super Spartan" event in Temecula and returned looking like they'd been abducted and dragged behind a moving vehicle. Robyn had small scrapes all along her arms and legs, and Albert had a gash in his stomach that looked like the alien from *Alien* had burst out of it. They'd both been beaten up by mean "Spartans," men with foam-padded sticks who seemed to be particularly enraged by the color pink. It was awesome, Robyn said.

I'd take her word for it. I wasn't sure how getting beat up by men with bats was awesome, or how it was exercise, but I was desperate. I needed something to do to restore my sanity, my endorphins, and my social life. To get me out of my home office and back into society.

The next obstacle race in California was two days and 350

miles away. I signed up hoping for a miracle; it would be the first time I'd tried to jog since my last five-mile outing landed me in the doctor's office, the girl with feet on fire.

Survivor Mud Run

LATHROP, CALIFORNIA
APRIL 21

I'm standing in the dirt on a farm a few miles south of Stockton, California. It's not a cow farm, though it smells like one. Dell'Osso Family Farm it's called, and it looks like a place kids would beg to visit, a Pollyanna-esque carnival visible from the 5 Freeway.

A three-tiered ropes course looms in the middle of the property, flanked by a zip line and a giant bouncy dome. There's a miniature city, complete with a "country store" and stands for all kinds of fair foods: corn on the cob, funnel cakes, giant smoked turkey legs. And then there's dirt. Acres and acres of flat dirt with hardly a sprig of grass poking through. This place certainly doesn't look like a venue for an endurance event, but today that's exactly what it is.

"Who's ready for the Survivor Mud Run?" an announcer yells from the start line as Lady Gaga's "Born This Way" pumps on loudspeakers. It's a few minutes before 9:00 AM, and it's almost 90 degrees outside.

The first wave of three hundred people funnels through the start chute. There's a hefty middle-aged couple wearing Superman underwear over tight spandex unitards. Women in neon-green shirts that say MAN UP, NANCY! A young man with an asymmetrical haircut whose motto seems to be "leave no skin unpierced!"

This is not my crowd. Maybe 10 percent of these people look like athletes. The rest look like they popped out of a time capsule buried just before Halloween in 1985. But I reserve judgment. I'm here on a mission, and right now that mission is to find my newly adopted team of gay Asian and Pacific Islander softball players from San Francisco.

I met two of Team Xtreme's fourteen members at the Hampton Inn pool last night when Jimmy and I jumped into the chlorinated water in an attempt to rid ourselves of the cow stink that had seeped into our skin after a five-hour drive up the 5 from Los Angeles with no air conditioning. John, a kind man who looked about thirty-three and had a tattoo of a bird on his inner arm, took pity on me for having no friends to run with and invited me to join his group. Now I have fourteen teammates to take on this bastardization of a 5K with me.

Jimmy is on hand as an unsanctioned event photographer, ready to document my triumphant return to sports and socializing. As a token of encouragement, he gave me his spikes from high school cross country so my shiny new Brooks Adrenalines wouldn't get sucked away in a mud vortex.

So here I am, at a farm, standing in the hot sun, wearing an old black Speedo bikini top, spandex triathlon shorts, and shoes that are three sizes too big, searching for Team Xtreme among the three hundred people lining up to start in the second wave at 9:15 AM.

When I stop walking to adjust the green bandanna on my head, a pair of smiley women who appear to be in their midfifties start talking to me. They both look like my mom. They're wearing matching pink-and-purple outfits, and they tell me they're nervous. This race is going to be hard! they say. They smile. I smile back to be polite and to stop myself from questioning why I'm here. I'm not even sure a "mud run" can be called an athletic event. It's really more of an excuse to drink beer, and nobody needs to drive five hours to do that. But before I can think any further about my decision, I spot the bird tattoo.

John and several of his team members give me double high-fives. It makes me feel a little better. Then we circle up and, on three, we all shout, "Hunger Games!" I don't know why.

"Ten seconds," says the announcer. "Five, four, three, two . . ."

A few minutes after crossing the start line, Team Xtreme and I face the first obstacle: a big, sloshy, fetid mud pit with flags strewn a few inches above the surface. Our objective: crawl under the flags. I jump in and immediately swallow mud. It mixes with my snot and dribbles thick brown globs of gooberous dirt down my chin. I no longer want Jimmy to document this. I don't even want him to *see* this.

I dive headfirst down a waterslide and jog across open farmland until I hit a small field of tires. A girl who looks about my age and her male teammate pass me as I carefully place my clown feet in the rubber holes. Turns out she's the comedian.

"Hey, boys, why don't you come get me after the next obstacle," she says to the handsome EMTs as we jog by. I don't want her to get ahead of me, but I can't break away from her. The obstacles are spiking my heart rate and sapping speed from my legs.

We walk over balance beams and lift ourselves over chest-high walls. We climb over a fourteen-foot-tall rope web and muscle across monkey bars. We slosh through a long mud pit and scramble up and over hay bales. I don't feel like I'm exercising, though I'm sucking air and people are passing me on every obstacle.

And then comes the coup de grâce. A string of back-to-back obstacles placed just before the finish line and in plain view of cheering friends and family members. I struggle to hold a net above my head as I slide through the mud below it. Then I scoot over plastic rods and hesitantly enter a drainage tube that induces mild claustrophobia.

A final dive into another mud pit seals the deal. I deliriously wander across the finish line and almost black out. That last sequence of obstacles has driven my heart rate to its max, and I have to bend over to bring it back down.

Team Xtreme funnels in beside me.

"That was so awesome!" I blurt out to them, elated. I've never been so excited about running a twelve-minute mile in my life—and my Achilles don't hurt. It's a miracle. Jimmy takes a group photo, and we all high-five and exchange emails.

As I walk to the showers—hoses on a platform set up over a ditch—my mind gets stuck on obstacle courses. I'd known about mud runs and Tough Mudders and Spartan races, but I'd written them off as events for the untrained masses, as preludes to an afternoon of drinking. Maybe that's exactly what they are, but this event was certainly enough of a challenge to earn a free beer. (Although for a $60 entry fee, that Belgian ale is far from free.)

Then it hits me again, that feeling that I could do so much better at this if I tried. But what is *this?* Can I even compete in it? What's the ultimate goal of an obstacle course racer? A world championship?

Welcome to the fantastic, strange, and scandalous world of obstacle racing, where nothing is what it seems.

2

The Mud Kings

WILL DEAN IS the Kim Jong-un of obstacle racing. The thirty-three-year-old boy-faced Brit is secretive, pugnacious, and tyrannical. He's also the reason obstacle racing became the fastest-growing endurance sport ever seen in the United States.

Flashback to early 2009, when Dean was a second-year student at Harvard Business School. Back then, it would've been hard for anyone to find a mud run close to home, not to mention one that presented an actual endurance challenge.

Serious athletes burned out on running or triathlons might have turned to adventure racing instead, while weekend warriors could have made a pilgrimage to Joliet, Illinois, to participate in the world's first Warrior Dash, a "mud-crawling, fire-leaping, extreme 5K run from hell" that debuted in July 2009 with two thousand participants.

If you had a mountain bike, you could have waited for

one of thirteen Muddy Buddy events to pass through town. In those races, competitors take turns running and riding a bike on a six-mile course strewn with military-style obstacles. That series started in 1999 and dominated the skimpy obstacle course market for nearly a decade.

But aside from Muddy Buddy and a handful of home-grown races, Americans aching to get dirty had to join the military or go to summer camp. And athletes who wanted to race an obstacle course event that would grant them the bragging rights of a marathon or triathlon were flat out of luck.

That's where Will Dean comes in.

According to official statements released by his regime, Dean is a former counterterrorism agent for the British government. He spent five years chasing bad guys through the Middle East and Southeast Asia before he decided he'd had enough and would like to get an American MBA, and he'd like to get it at Harvard, presumably because his chances of getting blown up by a mortar bomb or sniped on campus in the class of '09 were much lower than at his day job.

His employment history, of course, is unverifiable, as his former employer is also notoriously secretive. A call to the British Ministry of Defense will elicit the following response from a perfectly proper press officer: "I cannot verify that information for obvious reasons." Obvious reasons likely being that terrorists Dean might've dealt with would target him upon learning his identity.

Moving on, according to Dean's approved life story, he must've found Harvard's curriculum undemanding, as he had a lot of time on his hands that he decided to fill running marathons and triathlons, two sports that were experiencing a surge in popularity in 2008 and 2009. He also squeezed in a

Muddy Buddy and a trip back home to England to check out a strange decades-old 15K race called Tough Guy.

Neither swim-bike-run nor 26.2 impressed Dean. In fact, he found those sports quite repetitive and boring, a revelation that led him to what entrepreneurs love to call "the aha moment," or the point in time when they dream up the next big thing.

Dean submitted a proposal to Harvard's annual Business Plan Contest, the winner of which scores $25,000 in cash, among other prizes. Dean thought he'd nailed it with a plan for a business called Tough Mudder.

In the plan, he claimed he could attract five hundred people to run a ten-mile course covered in mud and man-made obstacles. He wanted to put the fun back in endurance sports, starting by reinjecting a sense of adventure and camaraderie. He wanted to design an event where competitors had to help each other toward the finish line.

His professors thought he was nuts. Who the hell is going to do that? they asked. More important, who the hell is going to *pay* to do that?

Dean didn't win the contest, but he stuck with his plan, putting on the first Tough Mudder at a ski resort near Allentown, Pennsylvania, on May 2, 2010, a seemingly arbitrary date. The course was seven miles long, and 4,500 people paid upward of $100 to navigate its freezing ponds, muddy hills, and flaming piles of straw.

The event was a huge success, garnering coverage in the *New York Times* and putting Dean's little Brooklyn-based company of six employees and two interns—all in their twenties—on the map. Three more events followed in 2010, banking Tough Mudder more than $2 million in revenue right off the bat.

Dean was certainly on to something, but he and his Tough Mudder series weren't alone. Just two weeks after the first Tough Mudder debuted in Pennsylvania, another event began in Burlington, Vermont, that would become Tough Mudder's greatest nemesis.

To the regular Joe, it might've looked like a fluke, like some big, bearded fitness fairy sprinkled enchanted mud droplets over the northeastern United States in May 2010, sprouting two of the fastest-growing endurance events of all time within two weeks of each other. But Dean's nemesis is no regular Joe—he's Joe De Sena.

If Dean is the Kim Jong-un of obstacle course racing, then De Sena is OCR's Teddy Roosevelt, minus the "speak softly" mantra, plus a bucketful of intimidation.

The forty-two-year-old is tough and determined. He's passionate about the outdoors, hard work, and even harder exercise. He doesn't take crap from anyone and absolutely does not tolerate whining. America's gone soft, he thinks. Our lives are easy. Nothing we do is a true mental or physical challenge.

To be fair, De Sena's definition of a "challenge" may be skewed. The man's physical accomplishments could put the world's most athletic overachievers to shame: he once completed twelve Ironman triathlons in one year.

Another time he did a 100-mile run, an Ironman, and the 135-mile Badwater Ultramarathon—all in one week. In a popular photo of him, De Sena is glaring at the camera from under the hood of a red North Face jacket as he makes his way through Alaska's 350-mile Iditasport Ultramarathon.

De Sena was a Wall Street banker managing a portfolio that brought in $50 million in revenue when he had his aha moment: he should create the hardest endurance event on the

planet. Life in the city was too cushy, and those other events
he'd done just didn't cut it. He needed a better challenge, and
he and his racing buddies were the only people who could
create one worthy of their own participation.

They dubbed their event the Death Race, and it was unlike anything the endurance world had ever seen. There was
no course map, no official distance to cover, no aid. Competitors were just as likely to find themselves memorizing Bible
verses or chopping onions as crawling under barbed wire or
scaling wooden walls. De Sena and seven equally masochistic friends set up the course near his home in Pittsfield, Vermont, and gave it a trial run in 2004. Then De Sena opened
the Death Race to the public.

If the event's strange tasks and fear of the unknown didn't
completely mess with competitors' heads, De Sena's pre-race
emails did. "Don't do this race," he'd write. "You're not good
enough. You may die." Despite the ominous warnings and advertised 90 percent failure rate, 87 people signed up for the
race in 2010 — a 690 percent increase over 2005.

De Sena realized there might be a market for this type of
event if athletes didn't have to cover more than forty miles, as
Death Race competitors often did. He decided to tone down
the distance but not the mind games, in order to bring the
"never say die" spirit of his beloved Death Race to the masses.
And so the Spartan Race Series was born with events ranging
from three to twelve miles long. The first Spartan race kicked
off in Burlington, Vermont, on May 16, 2010.

Neither De Sena nor Dean could've predicted what would
happen next.

Obstacle course racing exploded, covering the globe with
muddy competitions. With little more than $8,000 in Face-

book advertising, Tough Mudder sold out nearly every event it held, hosting more than 10,000 competitors in a single weekend. The Spartan Race Series sold out too, capping its fields at 6,000 entrants. And as for that Warrior Dash, which started with one race in 2009 and targeted everyday folks looking for some weekend fun, its events were selling out, with more than 20,000 costumed warriors at each one.

Something about obstacle course racing struck a nerve with people everywhere, and these events scrambled to expand fast enough to feed the world's voracious appetite for dirt. The astronomical rate of growth of those three series alone quickly surpassed that of marathons and triathlons.

In just its third year of existence, obstacle racing hosted more than 1.5 million competitors. That's a 3,558 percent increase over the estimated 41,000 people who competed in 2010. In that same time period participation in half-marathons, dubbed America's fastest-growing running distance, rose 34 percent, from 1.38 million finishers to 1.85 million.

By 2013 more than 3 million people had run an obstacle course. As the world's largest running race series, Warrior Dash earned sponsorship deals with Monster Energy and Miller Lite. Tough Mudder reached its one-millionth registration and scheduled fifty-three events, with sixty planned for the next year. Spartan Race hosted sixty races and more than 650,000 competitors across the globe. And those three brands were far from alone in the obstacle course market.

Obstacle-laden races sprang up across the country. No event producer's portfolio was complete without some type of mud run, often advertised with one flagship obstacle and a post-race beer garden. That Survivor Mud Run I did sold out with 13,000 participants, and the race director planned to expand his series from eight events in 2012 to fourteen the next year. Filling a few ditches with water was quickly becoming a viable career option for hundreds of people, and jumping into those ditches became a favorite pastime of millions more. Even Kim and Khloé Kardashian did the NorCal Survivor Mud Run in 2014.

Advertisers quickly took note of the phenomenon, but endurance athletes and their outfitters seemed particularly enamored of two events: Tough Mudder and Spartan Race.

Tough Mudder immediately positioned itself as a team challenge, squashing all efforts to label it as a race. (Seriously—don't call it a race or you'll tick off Will Dean.) Camaraderie was in Dean's business plan, after all, and he achieved it by making his events untimed, uncomfortable, and virtually unfinishable without help from fellow Mudders. A genius marketing strategy bolstered by the claim that the courses were "designed by British Special Forces," because what's more hard-core and team-oriented than the military?

All Tough Mudder events are ten to twelve miles, with thirty-five obstacles and an average finishing time of three and a half hours—just long enough to be memorably epic, but short enough to be a realistic goal, not unlike running a marathon.

Athletes are guaranteed to face obstacles like Arctic Enema, a neon-colored ice bath resembling radioactive waste; Everest, a quarter-pipe covered in cooking spray; and the series' crown jewel, Electroshock Therapy, a field of dangling live wires advertised as being juiced with 10,000 volts of electricity.

Some obstacles are only fun if you're suffering through them with friends; others require teamwork to conquer. And to drive home the point that this is a team event, before anyone is allowed on the course, each Mudder must recite the following pledge:

> As a Tough Mudder, I pledge that I understand Tough Mudder is not a race, but a challenge. I put teamwork and camaraderie before my course time. I do not whine—kids whine. I help my fellow Mudders complete the course. I overcome all fears.

This "leave no man behind" mantra, combined with the promise of a post-event beer garden, quickly made Tough Mudder the race of choice for hundreds of thousands of people, including American soldiers, and created an instant fanaticism that endurance outfitters could not ignore.

Tough Mudder made a reported $70 million in revenue in 2012, thanks in part to a sponsorship deal with a leading sports company, Under Armour, worth a rumored $2 million to $3 million. And in 2013 the company's projected revenue was $100 million, partially owing to expanded operations abroad in the United Kingdom, Japan, Australia, Germany, and South Africa. The event appeared on NBC's hit reality show *The Biggest Loser,* and weatherman Al Roker even got in on the action when he and his cohosts conquered Arctic Enema and Everest on the *Today* show.

The Spartan Race Series positioned itself differently. "Designed by Royal Marines," a Spartan event is a race, not a mud run. (Seriously—don't call it a mud run or you'll tick off Joe De Sena.) It fills the athlete's need for individual competition. Sure, teams can race too, but these events are timed and athletes are ranked in a points system, with the top Spartans eligible for prize money at the end of each year.

While Tough Mudder excels at making people feel uncomfortable by dunking them in neon ice water or running them through fields of charged wires, Spartan races are known for being physically demanding and mentally twisted. Want to skip an obstacle? At a Tough Mudder there is no punishment. At a Spartan race you must do burpees — a push-up followed by a vertical jump. Thirty of them. See the finish line? At a Tough Mudder you run through those electric wires and straight into the cool embrace of a Dos Equis. At a Spartan race you get within inches of the finish line and are forced to solve a Rubik's Cube or hit a target with a spear before being allowed to cross. And you cannot escape the Spartans, those jacked-up dudes with foam-padded pugil sticks whose sole mission is to take you out. A Spartan race messes with your head and trashes your body, and people who want to compete for time can't get enough. They also don't always finish.

The series is divided into different distances, much like triathlons or running races, including the three-mile Spartan Sprint, eight-mile Super Spartan, and twelve-mile Spartan Beast. For particularly masochistic endurance athletes, there's also the Spartan Ultra Beast — a marathon-length Spartan race.

I had run only one obstacle race, but that was all it took. Something that had been snuffed inside of me lit back up. The desire to train was creeping back into my veins, and it was energizing. I imagined that becoming an obstacle racer now would be something akin to becoming a triathlete in the '70s, when the sport was newly invented, rules were virtually nonexistent, and input from a single racer, like me, could help shape the sport. It was a once-in-a-lifetime opportunity to be part of an endurance sports movement from the beginning, and I wanted in.

I started to map out a race plan. I'd run the Camp Pendleton Mud Run and the local Tough Mudder. I'd see what else I could find within driving distance, and to cap off an awesome summer of competition I would race the Spartan Ultra Beast in September. An obstacle race of that distance had never before been produced, making it irresistibly intriguing—something like running the very first Ironman. It would give me something to work up to.

Best of all, Robyn would do it all with me. We'd get to train and race together and go on an epic adventure that was long overdue. What could possibly go wrong?

REDONDO BEACH, CALIFORNIA

JUNE 1, SIX WEEKS AFTER THE SURVIVOR MUD RUN

When Jimmy gets home from work, I tell him I'm making the Ultra Beast my Ultraman for the year. He is not pleased.*

"You do realize you'll probably hurt yourself. Don't they make you run up ski mountains?" he says. "How much does it cost?"

"Two hundred twenty dollars. And I'm signing you up too—"

"You registered already?"

I suppose now would be a bad time to tell him I registered both of us for Tough Mudder SoCal as well. "I'm just signing you up for the Beast. It's a half-marathon, and it's on the same

---

* To be fair, my last great idea landed us in the middle of Wisconsin, sleeping in a house with two midnight-pasta-scarfing Norwegians after spending a full seven hours and twenty minutes face-planting down a cross-country ski trail.

course. I know you'll want to go, and you'll get bored just hanging out."

"Go where?"

"Vermont."

"Vermont!"

"It'll be fun! And besides," I mumble, "I sold a story about the race."

"You what?!"

I had indeed done just that. In an effort to make a living, I'd been pitching stories about all kinds of things to all kinds of people, and in a sick twist of fate the one that stuck was a story about the Ultra Beast: the first marathon-distance obstacle race ever staged. I said I would do the race—I signed a contract that said I would do the race. It was now my job to compete.

"You can't even run right now!" Jimmy says. "What makes you think you'll be able to run a freaking marathon in four months?"

"I felt okay at the Survivor run."

"A 5K!?"

"I'll be fine. I promise."

A week later, I'm in rehab. It's late May, and mornings are foggy by the beach in Los Angeles. The gloomy gray mist accentuates how much it sucks to be in physical therapy, like the sky is a giant, ugly mood ring.

"You need to shut it down," says Fred the therapist as he digs his fingers into my Achilles and the bottoms of my feet. I was cycling up Southern California's Mount Baldy in an attempt to get back in shape when it suddenly felt like my Achilles and the soles of my feet ripped apart—like my calves

were playing tug-of-war with my heels and using my Achilles
as the rope. Among the things I am not supposed to do from
this day forward: swim, bike, run, walk. What I am allowed
to do: go to rehab Monday, Wednesday, and Friday mornings
at 7:00.

There are other athletes, mostly in their thirties and for-
ties, and grannies and grandpas. The only thing that unites
everyone doing exercises in the big, open room on the top of
an office building is how defeated they look. Deflated. Like
their bodies have betrayed them and rehab is their last futile
attempt to fix whatever's broken.

I arrive optimistic anyway, willing to follow Fred's instructions exactly so that I can race the Ultra Beast like a pro, even
if that means I won't be training for a month. I promised
Jimmy I would shut it down like Fred told me to.

Fred groups his clients by injury to make a competition
out of our recovery. One murky morning he points to an older
woman doing heel raises in the corner next to a Bosu ball.
He tells me that she's a runner who also injured her Achilles.
Then he says she set herself back because she gardened too
much over the weekend. Point for me! I don't have a garden to
stand around in. Another morning he tells me she ran across
an intersection, and that's why she's not any better this week.
Point for her, I think. I'd rather have Achilles tendinosis than
get hit by a car, even if Fred does seem disappointed in her decision.

Although I enjoy the idea that I'm recovering more quickly
than my rival, the reality is that each trip to Fred is leaving me
more inflamed than the last. My Achilles are on fire, and after
only two weeks of therapy — just when I think nothing else
could possibly go wrong — all hell breaks loose. Now it's not
just my Achilles that are screaming. My knees swell up. My

right shoulder puffs out. It's like every part of my body is re-volting against the calf raises and wall squats and bridges Fred is making me do, and the inactivity I'm forcing them into. I physically cannot move.

"Maybe you don't want to race all of that crazy stuff you do anymore," my dad says on the phone, almost hopefully.

Fred tells me that sometimes you have to get worse to get better, so I decide to gut it out. I slink across the room to do the exercises he's prescribed, and as I stand one-footed on a wobble board, I speak with a woman who looks like Lisa Loeb—Lisa Loeb now, not when "Stay" came out—and is recovering from a back injury. I tell her I'm giving physical therapy one month. It sucks to be inactive for so long, I say, and nothing seems to be improving, but I have no other choice—I'm going to run the most epic obstacle race ever invented.

"Oh, honey," she replies. "Rehab is a long-term commit-ment. This is my third year coming, and I think I'm finally making progress."

Dr. W doesn't know what to do with me. My muscles have already atrophied. The athlete's quads and calves that had al-ways made toothpick jeans an impossible wardrobe choice have withered away, leaving behind a pasty, gaunt person I don't like seeing in the mirror.

"It's weird, right? That I got tendinosis of everything all at once?" I ask.

Dr. W nods, and back to the lab I go. A vampire's din-ner of blood flows from my left arm into several tubes. The results: I'm fine. Fabulous even. I'm still not diabetic, nor do I have rheumatoid arthritis (my Google-aided second self-di-agnosis). If only all of my patients had your cholesterol levels! Dr. W says. There's nothing more he can do.

I am mega-bummed. Ridiculously, wholeheartedly dis-
tressed. At least before, when I was tired, I didn't want to
work out. Now I desperately want to train, to become a bona
fide obstacle racer. I have about three months until the Ultra Beast, and I cannot move. So I do the only logical thing a
woman in my situation can: I blame Fred for my sorrows and
break up with him. I don't have many more tendons left for
him to inflame, and I can only imagine what he's told other
Achilles sufferers about my inability to heal under his care.
"Oh, she walked across her apartment today in socks! Dread-
ful! What a setback!"

I call his office.

"Hi, this is Erin. I'd like to cancel my appointment on
Monday."

"Okay, when would you like to reschedule?" his secretary
asks.

"Never."

"One second, let me get Fred."

Really? Can't we just quit seeing each other?

"Hello?"

"Hi, Fred, it's Erin, I've decided to try something different.
Thanks for your help." Ohmygoshthisissoawkward.

"Like what?"

Like what? What do you mean like what? It's over, Fred!
Let me go.

"Um . . . like a chiropractor?"

"Yeah, that's probably what you need."

"Okay? Thanks for trying to help."

"'K, bye."

In a final Hail Mary attempt to repair the tendonitis, I sign
up for shock-wave therapy treatment. The procedure is sim-

ple: a podiatrist will rub goop on my feet and Achilles, then zap them with a wand that shoots sound waves into my tissues to trigger a healing inflammatory response. Apparently, my body no longer has any intention of repairing itself and has given up on my Achilles without my permission. This, the podiatrist says, should fix me. Famous ultrarunners come in all of the time for this treatment. Like who? I ask. Not allowed to say. Patient-doctor confidentiality, you know. But they do come, and they do keep running.

Jimmy sits in a corner, unsure of what's about to happen. He recoils and covers his eyes when the first pulses enter my Achilles and I jolt in pain and begin to scream obscenities.

The doctor revels in my agony and Jimmy's squeamishness and turns up the dial on the machine, smiling like an evil mad scientist. Oh, you muthafrigginfruggatyfrack! I scream in full-on vulgarities, my voice filling up the small office's hallway. Then the pain subsides a bit. The doctor turns the machine off and tells me to walk around.

I stroll down the hall and peer into other patient rooms. The elderly men and women waiting their turn have apparently heard everything. They look out at me, wide-eyed, wondering what Dr. Footkenstein will do to them next.

At that instant, it feels like my feet are completely normal. Like I never had an injury in the first place. But by the time we get to the car the inflammation has set in again and I can hardly move.

Now what am I going to do? Jimmy and I would both like to know. So I hatch a new plan: I shall become an obstacle racer through osmosis.

I read blogs about obstacle races. I watch YouTube videos of Spartans and Mudders and Warriors and dream of the day when a race photographer will snap a photo of me—muddy and gloriously strong—leaping over fire.

But I can learn only so much from behind a computer screen. I need to breathe in fellow obstacle racers' sweat and observe their technique firsthand. I need to be a part of the action.

"I'm not doing a Tough Mudder," Jimmy says, standing in the front door in his work clothes. The only major obstacle race taking place near us before the Ultra Beast is Tough Mudder SoCal. I need to experience a hard-core event so I don't go to Vermont totally clueless. It was part of my original race plan, like entering a half-Ironman before doing an Ironman; it's supposed to be a confidence-boosting stepping-stone.

"Please?" I say. "It's the only way I'm going to get good at this." Jimmy still doesn't know that he's already registered.

"No way. I'm not getting shocked. That's stupid."

"Your mom's stupid."

"That is the most unoriginal joke in the world."

"Your mom's the most unoriginal joke in the world, and I bet she'd do Tough Mudder because she's not a wuss."

I'd like to think the yo mama joke made Jimmy cave, but it was actually peer pressure—from other peers. More specifically, from Jimmy's boss.

Last year Garrett and thousands of other SoCal Mudders ran toward their heated cars instead of the finish line after jumping into Arctic Enema while freak snow flurries fell on their heads. They were all hypothermic.

Garrett wanted to avenge his DNF (Did Not Finish), so he started recruiting coworkers as teammates for this year's event. Jimmy couldn't pass up the epic bonding opportunity. And he didn't want to be the only guy to show up to work on post-Mudder Monday without a coveted orange finisher's headband and captivating battle stories.*

Also, I got a phone call that gave Jimmy another purpose for participating other than the fear of social ostracism or eating his entry fee.

I heard you're really into this obstacle racing stuff, a friend told me. Well, get this: Tough Mudder's being sued.

Jimmy and I would go to Tough Mudder SoCal for recon.

---

* I finally told him he was registered after he decided on his own to run. He thought I was being helpful. Timing is everything.

3

Mouse vs. Mudder

IT'S A WARM, sunny day in Snow Valley, California. Scores of caped superheroes are milling about, turning this ski resort into somewhat of an outdoor ComicCon. Hundreds of Tough Mudder competitors are wearing homemade T-shirts. Skinny dudes have "Sun's Out Guns Out" scrawled across their chests. There's also the "Fast and Hard" squad, the entirely uninspired "Go F*** Yourself" mob, and the beefy, shirtless, twenty-year-old guys who seal the frat party vibe along with a keg toss and plenty of beer.

"If any of you got those bizarre gorilla-foot monkey-toed shoes, you will not finish any faster than anyone else. Those were a waste of your hard-earned money," the announcer yells.

I hobble to the beginning of the run, where an eight-foot wall separates would-be Tough Mudders from the actual start line. I watch a woman grab the top of the wall with her fingertips as the men behind her with race numbers scribbled across their foreheads look at each other, then shrug and shove their palms into her posterior.

Somewhere in that crowd is Jimmy. I have instructed him to mentally note the obstacles he faces and to remember as many race details as he can, from the ambiance to the attitude to how bad it hurts to get zapped like a giant bug.

I'd asked Jimmy how long he thought the course would take him so I'd know when to send in the guys wearing the AMPHIBIOUS MEDIC T-shirts. He had no idea. A normal half-marathon would take him around an hour and twenty-five minutes, but this is no normal half-marathon.

Hundreds of people who've made it over the wall stand shoulder to shoulder while a tape-recorded LeAnn Rimes sings the national anthem. Then a hype man begins a start-line ritual. He makes everyone crouch down and acknowledge the war veterans among them. He tells a story about how a wounded vet with one leg did this course, so you can too! The most important thing is teamwork! Not your time! Then a man stands on a step stool in front of the crowd. It looks like he has the Tough Mudder credo tattooed on his back—his entire back. No. Freaking. Way. It must be Sharpie.

All of the competitors turn to the human cue card and repeat the credo. Then Van Halen's "Right Now" pumps over the loudspeakers, everyone counts down the start like the New Year's Eve ball is dropping, and they're off!

And I marvel at the brilliance that is Tough Mudder. There are no expensive road closures. Pricey timing systems are chucked in favor of the camaraderie credo, which, incidentally, makes it impossible to verify the number of participants or to easily look up a fellow racer since results will never be posted. And this race in particular is held at a ski resort that could desperately use the money after a dry winter and likely cut Dean a killer deal. Genius, really.

I watch Jimmy sprint off into the trees, then I meander. Way up the mountain, runners shuffle up what looks like a near-vertical dirt slope, like ants scurrying to the top of an ant farm. Below that, Mudders slither across slick black tarps placed under short, dangling wires.

This particular part of the course has its own soundtrack, a symphony of cheers, humming electricity, zaps, yelps, and cursing. *Zap!* F*@K! Go, Dad! *Zap!* SH*T! You can do it, honey! *Zap!* FU*^ITY FU*^! Looking good! *Zap!* AHHHH, KELLY CLARKSON!

Every four-plus-letter word imaginable fills the air as competitors scream their way across Electric Eel, a surprise shock obstacle that reduces grown men to crawling, crying babies.

Closer to the finish line, spectators swarm around other super-engineered obstacles to watch runners eat it. Mudders fall into cold neon-green water when they fail Funky Monkey, an enormous set of monkey bars that slopes up to a point, then back down. The muddy rods are spaced one and a half feet across, and some of them twist, making it nearly impossible to cross.

Around the corner, Mudders line up to get a running start up Everest, a greased-up, fifteen-foot-tall quarter-pipe. The guys who conquer it alone run full steam ahead, lean in, grab the top, and muscle up. But most people slip right back down to the bottom unless they manage to nab an outreached hand that yanks them to victory.

Everest is rumored to have the highest failure rate of any Tough Mudder obstacle, but on this course that title might go to a much smaller, unintended impediment: a piece of rebar sticking out of the ground on a downhill stretch of the run. It reliably downs one spectator every two minutes for over half an hour until a merciful spectator breaks off some red trail-marking tape and ties it around the steel.

Thanks to that woman, thousands of runners will avoid the rebar. But they can't avoid the final, most storied obstacle in Tough Mudder's portfolio: Dean's unique selling proposition, Electroshock Therapy.

Hundreds of long, yellow wires dangle like tentacles from wooden scaffolds, pulsating with 10,000 volts of electricity fueled by what looks like an old, rusty car battery. Soon these wires will become a gathering place for spectators eager to make YouTube sensations of the Mudders who charge through, only to be immobilized midstride, then face-plant spectacularly in the muck.

Funny how the very obstacle that put Tough Mudder on the map threatened to be Dean's undoing. Dean's like the Zuckerberg of obstacle racing! my friend had said on the phone. Will Dean stands accused of stealing his entire business plan, including those electric shocks, from another Brit while he was a student at Harvard.

Tough Guy Limited filed the case against Tough Mudder and Will Dean about a month after Dean staged his first race in 2010 in Pennsylvania, and it was a doozy. The complaint read:

In June 2008, Defendant Will Dean ("Dean"), a student at Harvard Business School in Cambridge, Massachusetts, contacted William Wilson ("Wilson"), founder of Tough Guy Limited ("Plaintiff"), located in England, and told him that he was conducting a field study for course credit regarding various races conducted around the world. Dean intended to analyze the feasibility and logistics of establishing Tough Guy in the United States. Wilson agreed to assist Dean and to provide information about his business if such information was not disclosed to parties unrelated to the Harvard field study or utilized for any commercial purpose.

On October 2, 2008, Dean traveled to the United Kingdom to meet Wilson in person. Wilson presented Dean with a written confidentiality agreement, which Dean signed. The agreement stated that Dean "would not use for any commercial end whatsoever, or disclose to any person connected with Dean's Harvard field study, the information regarding Tough Guy."

Plaintiff alleges that Wilson provided Dean with information about his business such as competitor demographics; financial breakdowns of income and expenditure; history of expressed media interest and actual media exposure; web and media statistics; and site layout and costs.

In or about January 2009, Dean presented Plaintiff with a copy of a Harvard Business School field study report entitled "Tough Guy—Evaluating the US/International Opportunity." The Complaint alleges that following the completion of the report, Dean ceased communications with Plaintiff.

In February 2009, Dean, with his business partner Guy
Livingstone ("Livingstone"), allegedly began marketing,
promoting, and advertising a series of races called
"Tough Mudder" via a retail website and popular social
networking sites . . .
    Plaintiff alleges that Defendants' Tough Mudder race
is an attempt to replicate Tough Guy. The Complaint
avers that based on the information disclosed by Plaintiff,
Defendants designed, developed, advertised, marketed,
promoted, and implemented the Tough Mudder race.

Dean's lawyers responded swiftly. They filed a motion to
dismiss Tough Guy's thirteen-part complaint and hoped the
issue would quickly disappear.

In the meantime, Harvard Business School's Conduct Review Board was investigating Dean's interactions with Tough
Guy after the British company sent the same complaints to
the school's dean. Four faculty members and three students
were looking into the case, though Dean had already graduated about a year earlier, in June 2009. What they found was
troubling.

Dean's involvement with Tough Guy, an event held in
England eighty miles away from Dean's hometown of Sherwood Forest,* began as an independent student research project conducted during Dean's second year of school. Though
Dean denied any wrongdoing, the review board found several
emails sent to Tough Guy founder William Wilson in which
Dean had overstated the school's interest in his project, possibly in an attempt to gain Wilson's trust.

"The CRB is concerned about these specific instances of

---

* Yes, the same Sherwood Forest of Robin Hood lore.

dishonesty and misrepresentation," the board wrote. "They are wrong in their own right and they violate HBS Community Values." Dean, the board found, had repeatedly fudged information sent to Wilson. In one email, for example, Dean said he'd been out of touch because he was busy with midterm exams—during the first month of the semester.

After finding similar instances in which Dean had distorted the truth, the review board concluded that Dean's claims about many things could not be trusted. Like when Dean said medical conditions and a rehab routine required him to "put his plan to launch Tough Mudder upon graduation from HBS on hold and thus back out of an agreement to hire a fellow HBS student as a summer intern." The review board didn't look into that issue, however, since there was already sufficient evidence of Dean's dishonesty, the board decided, to warrant action.

Perhaps the most damning of that evidence was this: Dean registered the domain name toughguyusa.com in June 2008, months before he officially started his independent research project in the fall.

The Conduct Review Board placed Dean on alumni probation for five years, starting retroactively on his graduation date, for violating the university's standards for integrity, honesty, and accountability.

The move ostensibly shut off Dean's alumni benefits, like access to job boards and networking events. It would also help maintain the school's good name in the business community should Dean's misdeeds ever become public knowledge. "If other MBA students engaged in field-based research were to follow Will's example," the review board wrote, "the reputation of the School would be compromised and the availability of field-based research opportunities likely would suffer, as well."

Not long after Dean's sanctioning, an overwhelmed California judge transferred the *Tough Guy v. Tough Mudder* case to New York. The new judge ultimately granted Tough Mudder's motion to dismiss just one of Tough Guy's thirteen complaints. The other twelve would be hashed out in court. Tough Mudder could only hope the prying eyes of the Googling public would not discover the case and the company would have time to build a brand based on teamwork, camaraderie, and leaving no man behind.

Around the same time, the business magazine *Forbes* published Mike Ozanian's story entitled "Tough Guy Competition Gets Praise as Original and Superior to Tough Mudder." In the article, Ozanian notes that *Forbes* readers reacting to an earlier article accused Tough Mudder of copycatting Tough Guy.

A comment on the story signed by "Tough Mudder HQ," however, accuses Tough Guy of spamming the article with negative posts and making "repeated threats of physical harm to Tough Mudder employees and family based solely on the similarity of the two business models." Tough Mudder, the company's HQ continues, "does not consider Tough Guy UK a competitor as our nearest event is more than 4,000 miles from theirs. Apparently Tough Guy organizers feel they have something to gain from this behavior."

But when Tough Mudder expanded into the United Kingdom with three events in 2012 — two of them within eighty miles of Tough Guy — it became a direct competitor. The argument that they were "more than 4,000 miles" away was no longer valid; Tough Mudder was encroaching on Tough Guy's turf, and William Wilson was upset.

He was still hurt by Dean's betrayal, to be sure. But Wilson wasn't mad for the other obvious reasons, like having his idea turned into a lucrative global business that gave him no recognition and paid him no licensing fees. Nor, on an even smaller scale, did he seem concerned about Tough Mudder's potential to pilfer local customers.

Wilson was upset because the vision he had for obstacle racing's role in his community is lost in this newer, oranger iteration. The toughness and shock factor are there in the fire, the ice, the electricity. But the soul of obstacle racing — the purpose behind the arduous activity as Wilson invented it in 1986 — is not.

Anyone seeking to understand that purpose, or where the outrageous, imaginative idea for a flaming, freezing, electric event came from, will not find it on Tough Mudder's "About Us" page. They'll find it in the wild story of William Wilson, and why he prefers to go by "Mr. Mouse."

Mr. Mouse is a movie-perfect septuagenarian. The philosopher has all the eccentricities of *Chitty Chitty Bang Bang's* Grandpa Potts, including a white handlebar mustache that he grooms with a brush kept in his front pocket and captivating, though largely unverifiable, tales of adventure.

"I've lived some real horrors," Mr. Mouse says. "I've been tortured for a couple of years, thrown into a cell where you've got nothing at all except hope. That's when your true character comes out of yourself, you know."

His story, as he likes to tell it, begins when he was four years old and first dreamed of death, consumed by a fever that struck just before the first day of school. He felt the Holy Spirit by his side that day and has never forgotten the experience.

His mother was a caring Catholic woman, but his father,

Arthur, was a drunk with an unpredictable temper. If Little Billy came home late, he could expect a leather-belt thrashing, a jab with a hot poker, or a trip to the corner to become a human dartboard.

Arthur abused Little Billy's mother, menacing her with that hot poker and, once, putting her in a chair on top of a bonfire and attempting to light it. Little Billy often dreamed of killing his father, but Arthur wasn't his only concern; his hometown of Wolverhampton had some rough patches ruled by gangs.

On Saturday mornings, Little Billy had to push a pram a mile uphill through three different gang territories to gather coke — a cheap derivative of coal — to heat his family's house. The Hill Street gang would try to push his pram back down the hill, pleased when the coke spilled out of it and Little Billy had to reload it all by hand. But the Stafford Street gang was much more cruel, preferring "torture, teasing, and penance forfeits" to the amateur escapades of the Hill Streeters.

Once, when Little Billy was eight years old, the Stafford Street gang captured him and marched him to Bone Mill Lane, where there was a railway bridge. They tied Little Billy's hands to the tracks. When he saw the train approach from around a bend, Little Billy rolled out of harm's way, letting the wheels cut his ties. He wiped his hands off in the grass, returned to his pram, and pushed it straight through the Stafford Street gang with ne'er a murmur from the little terrors.

He often dreamed of leaving home to escape his father, but Little Billy stayed to protect his mum. Once, when he was twelve, he tried to choke his dad to death by pushing Arthur's false teeth down his throat while he was sleeping. But Little Billy's mother rushed in to save him, so Little Billy decided to

set off on a twenty-four-day adventure, leaving home to explore neighboring villages, including one where a "kindly old
farm lady" fed him in return for some help with her chickens.
Little Billy held the poultry as she chopped off their heads,
then chased down their wiggling headless bodies.

When he was fourteen, he was finally big enough to stand
up to his father directly, delivering Arthur a punch square in
the face. And when Billy was eighteen, he came home on his
first leave from the British Army after fighting in colonial dis-
putes on the Arabian Peninsula and in Cyprus. His mother
had a scarf around her neck, and when Billy removed it, he
found finger marks and bruises underneath.

"I went to kill him with my bare hands," Mr. Mouse's account of the matter reads. "He had a knife. I dived at him and
crashed through the front door. I punched him, avoiding the
knife thrusts as he danced around."

The police arrived and took Arthur to the hospital's mental ward, where he underwent electroshock treatment that
turned him into "a cabbage in a wheelchair," effectively end-
ing the battle between father and son.

"I had as bad a childhood as anyone," says Mr. Mouse.
"But it didn't make me mad. I became a real tough guy — that's
where the name came from. It affected me because then I've
spent my life looking after everybody else's kids, trying to put
them on the straight and narrow. So it affected me in a way
that I created what is Tough Guy." Billy emerged from his trials a stronger person, and he hoped to help other people do so
too, including society's castoffs, underprivileged, and war veterans.

"We all have depression, periods of post-traumatic stress,"
Mr. Mouse says.

We all have periods where we're low. I get into those periods where I reach the depths of despair. I get into these bits of the mind, and then I get in deeper so I can see what it's like at the bottom of the pit. That way I can help people. And once you're in there—once you're in despair—you start feeling sorry for yourself, and that takes you in deeper, and deeper, and deeper. And then you better find that chink of light to crawl back out. You've got to find that escape from it.

So that's the stuff I teach through Tough Guy: how do you get out of it? We take you into the depths of despair—the underwater tunnel. There's real fear in there and you can't breathe and if you do you breathe water, and that's a test. That's a big test of life, that is, and you get through it. So there's a lot about being a Tough Guy that's much more than just the physical. You've got to do things with your mind. Meditation. Train your mind. You've got to face life completely.

Mr. Mouse wanted to help people break through whatever mental barriers might be keeping them from living full, rich lives. But how? Running, Mr. Mouse believed, was the answer. People share happiness when they run.

Mr. Mouse became enamored with the marathon boom in the early 1980s and found a hero in Fred Lebow, cofounder of the New York City Marathon and president of the New York Road Runners club from 1972 to 1994. Lebow lived a famously spartan lifestyle, giving all he had to the sport of running and taking only enough money in return for food.* Le-

---

* Perhaps Lebow didn't even take that much. He had an "always-empty" refriger-

bow's marathon, Mr. Mouse believed, transformed New York City from a cold, uncaring concrete island into a happier, friendlier place.

With that inspiration from across the pond, Mr. Mouse got involved in establishing the London Marathon and a British athletics association. And when he felt that running was becoming boring and the politics of running too tedious, he looked to his farm of rescued horses in Wolverhampton and challenged himself to create something out of the fields. Something that would help the community and teach lost souls to reclaim their lives by facing death. That something he created was Tough Guy, tagline: "The Safest Most Dangerous Event in the World."

In 1986, the year the first Tough Guy was held, Billy Wilson adopted the name Mr. Mouse "because you can only teach people if you are humble," he says. "So I wanted to be the humblest person, so I said well I'd better find a nickname. So I chose the mouse, which is the most humble of all creatures."

That inaugural event drew 103 hearty competitors who ran up a hillside, forded a stream, and waded through a swamp. When they finished, all bloodied and filthy, they smiled at Mr. Mouse and said, "That was fantastic! It's like being a child again!"

Mr. Mouse was on to something. Each year he added another challenge to instill fear in his competitors as they ran across the Killing Fields: Vietcong Tunnels; the Stalag Escape, a barbed-wire crawl named after German POW camps; the

---

ator, according to the founding publisher of *New York* magazine, George Hirsch, who wrote a tribute to his longtime friend published on the *New York Times*'s marathon blog. Lebow, Hirsch wrote, organized the first NYC Marathon in 1970 "with money from his own pocket for soft drinks, safety pins and cheap watches for the winners."

Tiger, two twelve-meter-tall frames covered with cargo nets and slung over electric fences charged with more than enough power to stun a bull; and Hanging Electric Jellyfish Tentacles, dangling wires charged with enough electricity to topple a grown man. (Worthy of note: In Tough Mudder's official video for the company's third event, held in New Jersey in 2010, Will Dean called his electrically charged dangling wires Jellyfish Tentacles. That Tough Mudder obstacle is now known as Electroshock Therapy.)

But Tough Guy's popularity didn't really explode until 2000, the year of Jesus's two-thousandth birthday. "To commemorate the torture of the original Tough Guy," Mr. Mouse's promotional pamphlet read, "every entrant will sign up as a Jesus Warrior. Each competitor will simulate the Passion and carry a huge cross to Calvary." The odd Asian or Jew would be allowed to carry a tree instead.

Mr. Mouse built five thousand crosses for the event, and the Church of England quickly condemned the crucifix-carrying challenge, saying it was in poor taste—the worst possible taste. Utterly tasteless. Tough Guy had never had so many entrants, and the event never stopped growing after that, despite one man's hypothermia-induced death at the Jesus Warrior race.

Mr. Mouse, consequently, needed a workforce. Building five thousand crosses and digging ditches are no easy tasks. He now employs twenty-two people, seven of whom couldn't get a job anywhere else, he says. He makes it a point to hire vulnerable souls—lads who've done time in prison, victims of physical and emotional abuse, and the mentally handicapped. He calls his 150-acre residence the Mr. Mouse Farm for Unfortunates, and through his event he raises money for charities that help soldiers and money for his farm, where he tries to employ the unlucky local adults and kids.

His own children, a daughter, Tracey, and two sons, Sean and Mitchell, were already adults by the time their father invented Tough Guy. Tracey eventually married Andy Taylor, guitarist for the hit '80s band Duran Duran, and her brothers wound up tagging along on Duran Duran's world tour.

But Mr. Mouse was not interested in any of that glamour and fortune. What kills him today, he says, are those USA-based rogues—crooks!—who, out of greed, have stolen by deception his intellectual rights and copycatted his beloved event to make millions of dollars. His lawyers liken his case to that of Mark Zuckerberg and Facebook: another Harvard brat striking it rich off of somebody else's idea.

For a second I forget all about Tough Mudder's scandalous background and stand in awe of the monster frat party surrounding me in Snow Valley. How many of these neon-span-dexified Mudders would care that the idea for this get-to-gether might have originated with a mustachioed old Brit? That Will Dean had to pay Mr. Mouse $725,000 in a confidential settlement? Or that he never signed the MBA Oath, a voluntary pledge for graduating MBAs and current MBAs to "create value responsibly and ethically," started by two of his '09 classmates? Heck, once Tough Mudder began its explosive trajectory upward in both brand recognition and revenue, Harvard Business School didn't even seem to care that Dean was on academic probation; the school's entrepreneurship club welcomed him as a speaker at its annual conference in 2012.

Something tells me the young men up onstage wearing

pink bras and pink camo booty shorts wouldn't mind if the devil himself had invented Tough Mudder; they just want to party.

I plop down on a bale of hay wedged between Electroshock Therapy and a tank. A real live tank guarded by men in camouflage. Real live military fatigues covering their heads, arms, and legs, not the pink stuff I saw earlier. And there I wait. A muscled young guy begins to talk to me, but as soon as I tell him I'm waiting for "my husband," he turns to the girl in a bikini behind me and forgets I'm alive.

I turn back to Electroshock Therapy. The contraption somehow fills my heart with happiness. It's amazing that there's still an event out there of this magnitude that requires participants to take responsibility for themselves, albeit by signing a four-page liability waiver. If you hurt yourself, it's your own damn fault.*

Finally, a lone man comes running through the wires. He doesn't eat mud, and I'm mildly disappointed. But before I start to feel bad that I wanted to see him collapse, a few groups charge through the cold mist of a snowmaking machine and into the final obstacle. People drop left and right. Some teams hold hands—then they all go down together. When one woman tumbles, she refuses to get back up. She flattens herself against the ground in a futile attempt to distance her body from the shocks, then starts to cry.

Eventually, the obstacle masters shut off the electricity, drag her out, then start it up again. Superheroes and crossdressers splatter me with mud when they crumple by my feet. And just when I turn to ask the old man sharing my hay bale who he's waiting for, out of the corner of my eye I see Jimmy

---

* Or maybe it's not. See chapter 10.

catapulting face-first down a slope of hard-packed dirt. One of the very last wires got him good.

Tough Mudder HQ is a block from the water in Brooklyn's trendy DUMBO (down under the Manhattan Bridge overpass) district. Soon the company will move to a larger space around the corner in the MetroTech Business Improvement District, a twenty-five-block area that's home to a diverse group of businesses, including 3D printing start-up MakerBot and health insurance giant Empire Blue Cross Blue Shield.

But for now Tough Mudder's corporate operation occupies about five rooms in a blockwide concrete building that also houses the posh online marketplace Etsy. Perhaps that's where Tough Mudder got the personalized floor mats that designate which third-floor rooms in this industrial-looking office building are theirs and the flame-logoed pillows scattered around the break area.

Jane Di Leo, Will Dean's PR manager, makes working for Tough Mudder sound a lot like attending college orientation for eternity. She talks about quarterly retreats to a cabin in the Catskills and officewide color wars complete with balloon tossing and scavenger hunts. About group lunches, buddy systems, and the importance of each hire's "culture fit." About monthly discussions of Harvard Business School case studies, including one about Starbucks's morph into a brand set on world domination. "I've never been bored, and we never stop learning," Jane says with a sweet smile.

Each Tough Mudder room is painted a bright color. Red for accounting, green for HR, the company's signature orange everywhere. Bikes lean against the hallway walls, a red Raleigh Pursuit, an old Kona rig. Young twentysomethings dressed in short shorts and T-shirts, summer dresses and flip-flops, wave from inside the offices. They seem happy. In fact, every single company review posted on Glassdoor.com, a career site where employees can rate their companies and bosses, is glowing. Dean even has a 100 percent approval rating—higher than that of, well, every CEO on Glassdoor, including the CEO of Starbucks. Never mind that those reviews were all posted on the same day. Or that one reviewer wrote: "Management required everyone to right [sic] positive reviews on this website."

Jane talks about teamwork and a culture of camaraderie governed by the Tough Mudder employee credo: "Be good to people." It's different from the one that participants repeat: "I do not whine; kids whine." "Be good to people" is the part of the ten-point employee doctrine that sticks out, something akin to Google's mantra "Don't be evil."

Mr. Mouse would like the credo, but he would never have created all this: setting up shop in the heart of American pop culture; employing recent college grads and poor spellers rather than society's true unfortunates; studying the missteps and triumphs of global brands to guide the construction of an empire.

It takes hubris to shoot for world domination; it's not a role the humble seek.* It also takes a special talent that few people have but many admire.

Dean's ability to grow Tough Mudder into a multimillion-dollar, multinational brand in just three years has earned him praise as a visionary businessman. Professional services firm Ernst & Young named Dean its "Outstanding Entrepreneur

---

* Unless you're a "Level 5 leader," a term Dean surely learned at Harvard. As business consultant Jim Collins wrote in the *Harvard Business Review,* a Level 5 leader is "an individual who blends extreme personal humility with intense professional will." Collins claims that good companies are never transformed into great, enduring companies without Level 5 leaders at the helm.

of the Year" in 2013 "for his vision to create an innovative and spirited obstacle course that is now the premier adventure challenge series." The industry trade newspaper *Crain's New York Business* named Dean to its annual "40 Under 40" list in 2012, an accolade reserved for "business leaders who have proven themselves to be among the brightest and most talented" in the city.

Though it exposed flaws in Dean's character, Mr. Mouse's legal war had little impact on his business. In fact, Mr. Mouse is far from Tough Mudder's biggest problem. The greatest threat to the flaming orange empire lies 260 miles north of Dean's DUMBO operation in the mysterious Green Mountains of Vermont.

4

Vermonsters

THERE IS NO one at the inn. Just a piece of paper with my name and a room key on it.

The Trailside Inn is tucked away down a grassy hill, out of sight from a small and winding two-lane highway. There's a common room off of the hotel's entrance with a fireplace, a flat-screen TV, and tables made of thick wood slices dripping in wax. It looks like a place where burly men in plaid shirts would come to down beers and belt out bawdy tunes together after a long day outside. But not today: mine is the only car parked in the dirt lot.

Room 101 is a simple but charming space that smells of pine floors. There's not much to it. Just a full bed, a small rug, and two candies fashioned in the shape of maple leaves placed on top of a towel. That's not enough sugar to silence my growling stomach, so I leave my things in the room and drive north on Route 100.

The highway arcs through a forest of huge maple and beech trees and zigzags around a section where the original road disappears into the river. Past picturesque meadows and a big covered bridge that looks like it's straight out of *Yankee* magazine.

After almost ten minutes of driving, there's been no sign of a town. No stores, no gas stations, no people. Then suddenly, there's something: three homes that look like a tornado lifted them up, then pitched them down, are scattered by the river, off-kilter and abandoned. And across the street there's an old white building with BIKRAM YOGA printed on the side in red lettering, but it's dark inside.

Finally, past an old grassy graveyard with crumbling headstones and a small church, there's a general store—another old white building with a big front porch and a vacant dirt parking lot.

Inside, the store is rustic but remarkably upscale, stocked with produce from the local farm, organic and vegan cookies, bulk blueberry flax granola. Maple syrups, candles, socks, cards, moose puzzles. All beautifully displayed under a white chalk sign that says LIVE SIMPLY . . . SO OTHERS CAN SIMPLY LIVE.

"Can I help you?" says a man who pops up behind the counter. He's the first person I've seen all day, and it startles me. I almost drop a magnet with a moose on it that says "She left me for a guy with a bigger rack," and order a turkey sandwich.

"What brings you to town?" the man asks.

"I'm here to meet Joe De Sena," I say. What better way

to learn more about Spartan racing than from the series'
founder?

The man raises his eyebrows. "He kind of speaks in mono-
tone, doesn't he?" he says.

"I don't know, I haven't met him yet."

"Well, make yourself comfortable. There's napkins and water right over there," he says. Then he disappears behind the
counter, revealing a piece of paper tacked up on the wall wel-
coming Alexandra Marie De Sena into the world, 7 pounds,
19½ inches. She was born yesterday.

Just as I'm finishing up, a young man with a notebook sits
at the table next to me, then looks over and introduces himself. His name is George Heinrichs, he says, and he's headed
to the Spartan offices. We walk down the road together.

George recently graduated from Middlebury with a degree
in religion, and he ran the winter Death Race. This is his first
day working for Spartan Race. Joe owns the inn I'm staying
at, he says, as well as the inn he's staying at that's located on
the other side of town. His inn has a hot tub.

George walks right up to the Bikram Yoga building and
opens a back door with a sign on it that reads: NO SOLICIT-
ING OR CHIT CHATTING. THIS IS A PRIVATE BUSINESS.

This is it, George says. This is Spartan headquarters. A
back room in an old building that's half yoga studio, half office. This is the command center for Tough Mudder's biggest
rival.

Desks and computer screens line the space, and a giant
chalkboard covering the back wall hosts indecipherable scrib-
bles about race locations and supplies. A few boxes of Dial
Speed Foam sit in a corner near a wedding photo of a man
and his wife who are standing in front of a hot-air balloon.
The place is scrappy, if you can call a place that.

Three people are hard at work when George and I walk in. Before I have time to say hi to any of them, the phone rings and one of the guys answers it.

"It's for you," he says.

"Me?" What? I take the phone. "Hello?"

"It's Joe. Don't talk to those guys, you'll kill their productivity. We'll go for a hike later. I'm picking my wife up from the hospital."

"Okay?" I say.

"Put Jason on."

I pull the phone away from my ear, and the man who answered it takes it. He must be Jason.

"Um hmm," he says. "Uh huh. Okay."

He hangs up the phone.

"Do you have any questions?" Jason asks.

"I thought I wasn't supposed—"

"We can talk in here. He won't know. You can meet Joe tomorrow."

We enter a tiny, windowless office just off of the main room, and Jason shuts the door. He tells me he's in charge of the WODs—the Workout of the Day that's emailed to all Spartan participants, often with an inspirational quote attached, like "Perseverance is strength" (karate master Masutatsu Oyama), or "It's not the mountain we conquer, but ourselves" (Everest-conquering mountaineer Sir Edmund Hillary). The WODs are meant to inspire movement and to teach new athletes the basics of constructing a training plan.

"That's cool," I say. "How'd you get into doing that?"

Jason did Ironman Kentucky with a broken hip. He ran his hip into a stress fracture, then raced the Ironman anyway, hauling on the bike to make up for what was going to be a painful run. Then he DNFed after biking his way into heat stroke.

After the race, he needed to get away. A DNF is a tough thing to deal with, and he wanted a break from triathlon, racing, the whole scene in general. So he boarded a plane to Swaziland, Africa, to immerse himself in Swazi culture for a month.

On the last leg of his trip back to the United States, from Atlanta to New York, a flight attendant accidentally handed Joe's passport to Jason. So when Jason got home, he looked Joe up. He found out Joe was a Badwater Ultramarathon* finisher, which intrigued him, so he went to Manhattan to return the passport in person. The two chatted about their endurance feats, and Joe invited Jason to Pittsfield for the weekend, where he pitched Jason his idea for Spartan Race.

Jason was giving music lessons at the time—he's a classically trained guitarist—and was particularly interested in philosophy. He liked the idea of getting all kinds of folks engaged in sports. Jason and Joe both believed that most people hold themselves back from what they're capable of achieving; they wanted to rip people from their couches and show them nothing's impossible. They'd do it through free fitness education and a race structure similar to that of Ironman, without the financial barrier of the entry fee.†

Jason moved to Vermont to work on Joe's big idea, an enormous life change Joe had clearly inspired. Jason rented a house on a mountain and currently lives a monastic life there.

---

* The "world's toughest footrace," the Badwater Ultramarathon is a nonstop 135-mile run that starts in July in Badwater/Death Valley, California (elevation: 282 feet below sea level; average temperature: 116 degrees), and ends at Whitney Portals on Mount Whitney (elevation: 8,360 feet).

† Ironman holds races all over the world. The race season culminates in the Kona, Hawaii, championship event in October. The Ironman entry fee for each race is around $700.

No TV. No radio. Just books and silence. I wonder for a second if he was involved in decorating my room at the inn.

I don't want to go back to lonely room 101. There's a bit of daylight left, so I drive toward Killington Mountain. I want to see what the ski resort looks like. The hills around the hotel aren't too big—maybe the Ultra Beast won't be so hard after all. Maybe its gnarliness was all hype and no substance.

The road winds up and up and up, past small ski shops, closed restaurants, and townhomes. Then I see it. A beautiful mountain with ski lifts and grassy green chutes that glow in the evening light.

It's big. A big freaking mountain. Not Colorado big, but still. This ain't no tall frappuccino; this is a venti. The sight of it makes my Achilles ache and my stomach knot up.

On the way back to the inn, I grab some kind of coco-nutty cinnamon-roll-frostinged-chocolate-chippy dessert bar at a tiny supermarket and overhear the woman at the checkout counter speaking with another customer. Something about people around here dying and roads being dug up and fixed.

It's dark outside, and there are no lights on at the inn. The banjos from *Deliverance* play in my head as I throw open the front door, scurry to room 101, and lock the door behind me.

What a strange day. It was like Big Brother was watching my every move. Like I was in *The Truman Show* and the sandwich guy was deployed for the scene in the general store, then George showed up at just the right moment to take me to Spartan headquarters, then Joe called exactly as I entered the yoga building. It was truly bizarre, and now I'm stuck in an inn in the middle of nowhere, and all I can think of is that *someone* knows I'm here because *someone* knew everywhere else I've been today. But nobody is at the inn, and now I'm creeped out and—wait! What was that?

There's whistling in the hallway. Someone's in the hallway! When the tune gets as far away as possible, I poke my head out of the room, only to see the door at the end of the hall swing shut.

I dig my phone out of my bag, sit on the floor, and try to dial Jimmy. There's no cell phone reception. None. Not even a single bar.

I get up to make sure I bolted the lock on my door before I try out the Internet. Just as I put my hand on the deadlock—

Knock. Knock.

Holy s#*^!

"Who is it?" I say.

"It's Margaret."

I open the door to find local obstacle racer Margaret Schlachter, all smiles, standing in front of me in shorts and a black Killington Mountain School hoodie. I heard she was one of the sport's best competitors, so I emailed her from the general store to see if I could meet her. And here she is.

I try to play it cool, like I didn't almost just scream when she knocked.

"Come in!" I say. "You can sit on the bed."

Margaret enters and plops down, eager to talk about her obsession and all-time favorite sport. I check her out. She is one of the first hard-core female obstacle racers I've ever met. Considering that elite distance runners are lithe and elite swimmers have huge shoulders, I wondered if there's a body type that excels at obstacle racing. Judging from the specimen before me, I'd say that one must be on the short side, have killer quads and freckles, and be painfully nice to excel at this sport.

Before Margaret was an obstacle racer, she was an alpine skier and a lacrosse player. She just quit her job as head of admissions at Killington Mountain School to pursue OCR (the elites' preferred term for obstacle course racing) full-time. That makes her the world's first professional female obstacle racer. It's a title that requires no accreditation, just a big heart and even bigger guts.

Leaving a good post in private education was a gamble, she admits, but she recently turned thirty and who knows? Sometimes you just have to follow your heart and go for it. And right now her heart is telling her to race and to work on her website, Dirt in Your Skirt. Obstacle racing, she says, is becoming a legit sport. Legit in that some races are beginning to pay big money—as much as $15,000—to top finishers, and sponsorship opportunities for serious competitors should start opening up.

"Are you racing the Ultra Beast?" she asks.

"Racing is maybe not the right word for what I'll be doing, but yes, I'll be there," I say.

"Have you done any other Spartan races?"

"No."

For a second, this look flits across Margaret's sun-kissed face. This "well, it's been nice knowing you" look. But Margaret is too positive to let it stick. Then she says she better be going. She has a long drive tomorrow to a race in Virginia.

I don't want her to go. I want her to stay in my room and protect me from whistling Vermonsters, but I can't very well ask her to spend the night with me. That could be awkward.

Margaret walks into the dark, and I lock the door behind

her. I pray nobody cuts me to pieces in my sleep, then brush my teeth.

The water coming out of the tap is tinted red and tastes like blood.

A guy named Lee Goss, who may be the tallest man in the state, surely the tallest in Pittsfield, is waiting in the Spartan offices to talk business with Joe.

Lee comes with the Boston-based venture capital firm* that just invested in the Spartan races and is going to be the new Spartan president. It'll be Lee's job to take all of Joe's ideas and make them happen. Joe's an entrepreneur, and Lee loves entrepreneurs because they have so much creative energy. They do the impossible because they don't know they can't, Lee says. How nice it would be to have a Lee, I think, who can turn one's ideas into cash.

After forty-five minutes of sitting around, trying not to bother the Spartan employees, the "no chit chatting" door flies open and a man walks in. It's the man from the wedding photo on the wall.

"Joe!" Lee says, getting up to shake Joe's hand. Joe has a boyish face and a barrel chest. Crew-cut reddish-brown hair. He's maybe five-foot-ten, dressed in cargo shorts and a gray T-shirt with two swords crisscrossed on the front.

Joe walks over to the chalkboard. Then he makes a quick phone call. Then he looks at the chalkboard. Then at the phone.

---

* Raptor Consumer Partners, a Boston-based private equity firm founded by Boston Celtics co-owner James Pallotta, a billionaire and son of Italian immigrants. According to *Forbes,* the firm invested just under $10 million in Spartan Race.

"That's the good thing about ADD," he says. "I can never remember anything long enough to be upset about it. Follow me to the house. We'll talk there."

Joe drives his black Mercedes SUV a half-mile down the road before turning onto that beautiful covered bridge and crossing the White River to a fairy-tale property of rustic buildings and barns strewn across a big green meadow. It's a veritable estate. It even has a name: Riverside Farm.

As it turns out, Joe must have a lot of ideas, because he and Lee talk for hours while Joe's kids run around on an obstacle course Joe built in the meadow. Then they come bursting through the barn doors.

Jack, age seven, and Charlie, five, are wearing superhero shirts, and Charlie has Hulk hands on. It's getting close to kung fu lesson time with their Chinese instructor, who lives with his wife on one of Joe's properties. He teaches the kids for an hour every morning and evening. It keeps them disciplined, Joe says.

Catherine, Joe's three-year-old, says she's just there to keep an eye on Charlie to make sure he doesn't cry.

Joe's sixty-eight-year-old assistant, Sylvia, guards the breezeway that connects Joe's home to a big red barn. Another stranger Joe invited to live on his property, Sylvia has been working here for half a year—the warm half—every year since she was sixty-two. Sylvia met Joe one day when she and her husband were driving through town and stopped at the general store looking for a place to stay. Joe offered to put them up in the caretaker's cottage on his property. They offered to take him to and from the airport, and they've been friends ever since. Sylvia's husband does whatever handyman work Joe needs done, and Sylvia helps with everything else.

She can't gush enough about Joe or the farm. About the

beautiful weddings they host here and all of the different buildings dotting the thirty-acre meadow. There's the caretaker's home, the rehearsal dinner barn, the wedding barn, the bridal suite.

One year ago, Joe and Alex, Sylvia's husband, watched the river come up almost all the way to that bridal suite when Hurricane Irene flooded everything. Joe's covered bridge withstood the storm, but they were lucky. Other homes were destroyed. The river picked them up, tossed them about, and dropped them down by Route 100. Joe and Alex took out Joe's construction equipment and tried to help rebuild what was broken.

That same hurricane forced Spartan Race to shut down an event in Amesbury, Massachusetts. More than 150 runners showed up at 5:00 AM anyway to work out with Joe. The Spartan founders have run a Hurricane Heat at just about every event since as an untimed challenge that begins before the regular race and lasts about three to four hours, with Joe or another Spartan official putting their own twist on the course. (Think: burpees at every obstacle, course-long sandbag carry, or finish-line flutter kicks.)

Sylvia says she's never tried a Hurricane Heat, or a Spartan race for that matter. ("Girlfriend! I flunked phys ed!") But she appreciates the Spartan philosophy of living simply. "I've had it all," she says, "and I am happier here with the simple life."

It's 5:20 the next morning. I'm standing outside Joe's house in the dark in running shorts and an old triathlon shirt when I see George emerge from the cold fog. The three of us are going for a hike—the best way, Joe said yesterday after kids and business meetings gobbled up his time, to get his full attention.

Joe stumbles out of his door, bleary-eyed. Having a three-day-old child will do that to a guy. Of course I didn't sleep either. Not after hearing mystery footsteps in the hallway of a pitch-black inn at which I am still the only resident.

Joe grabs a 100-pound sandbag and begins to walk up the hill behind his property. This is certainly not how he would've pictured himself living a decade ago, he says—on his own farm at forty-three, with a beautiful hill to hike up every morning to watch the sunrise.

Joe grew up in Queens, New York. His dad was in construction, and his mom taught yoga. For as long as Joe can remember, he's always had to be doing something. When he wakes up, he's ready to go. He wasn't the best student, but he was already an entrepreneur by the time he got to high school, having started a swimming pool cleaning company when he was twelve or thirteen. He didn't have any equipment, so he took his dad's and let his father's pool turn green. A small price to pay to get his business going.

He kept it up while he went to high school and college in Ithaca, eventually garnering 750 accounts from Brooklyn to Montauk and employing twenty people. The thing about pools, Joe says, is that a lot of people who have them are wealthy. Financially successful. Several of Joe's accounts were for Mafia members who trusted little redheaded Joe to polish their tiles. And a lot of his clients worked on Wall Street. They admired Joe's work ethic and finagled him a job in finance, though he'd studied textiles at Cornell. He still works in finance as a managing director for the London-based brokerage firm ICAP, venturing into New York City almost every week.

Joe didn't know what to do with himself during his weekends off once he started working on Wall Street—his pool business had been a 24/7 deal. So he started racing. For him, it was a great escape from reality to do an event. And it was even more of an escape to compete in far-off places like Fiji, where he ran the Eco Challenge, a multi-day adventure race during which everything that could've gone wrong did.

Joe hands the 100-pound sandbag to George. We've been slowly jogging straight up a dirt road for about ten minutes.

Before the Eco Challenge started, a Fijian stole Joe's sneakers. So for the next eight days Joe ran the race in the rain through the interior of Fiji with bike shoes on. "Eight days in bike shoes—it's no joke!" Joe says.

When Joe got home, he and his friend Andy Weinberg went on an all-night snowshoe hike. They talked about the Eco Challenge and about the 50- and 100-mile ultramarathons Weinberg had been running. No doubt those runs were challenging, but the racers were getting soft, Joe and Andy thought, because they knew what to expect. Wouldn't it be cool to create a race that was just as exhausting mentally as it was physically? Like where they'd take a guy's bike seat off, so when he got out of the Ironman swim, he had no bike seat. What would the guy do?

Joe's always been interested in that reaction because he's been building businesses his whole life. So he's always looking for that employee or partner who will work hard. Who will just get it done, no matter what's thrown at them.

That revelation makes George's ears perk up. I think that's just what Joe wants.

That idea—that people should learn to persevere physically and mentally—was the beginning of what would become the Death Race and, eventually, the Spartan Race Series. Because, Joe says, what entered his mind in Fiji was that it's pretty cool to be with people who deal with whatever comes their way.

What enters my mind in Pittsfield is that Joe has a knack for racing in improper footwear.

A decade ago, around the same time as the Eco Challenge, Joe decided to jump into an event in Nantucket where there was an ocean swim. Joe's deathly afraid of sharks, so of course he had to do the swim. "I like to do things I don't like to do," he likes to say. So he did the point-to-point swim, got out on the other side, and was hopping barefoot from rock to rock when someone called to him, "You're gonna hurt your toot-sies."

Joe stopped hopping. His mother would've said something like that, he thought. He looked back to see that those words came from a beautiful woman named Courtney. He was smit-ten. The two began dating, and five months later Joe pro-posed by the Pacific Ocean during a Balance Bar twenty-four-hour adventure race. "Being married to me was going to be a long-distance event," he says. It seemed a fitting way to start their life together. Then there was the car crash.

Joe begins bushwhacking up the hill, picking blackberries along the way. When we near the top, Joe takes the sandbag from George and chucks it at me.

"You gotta deal with it," he says. Then George and Joe walk off.

I hold it still in my arms for a few seconds before the little grains of sand all migrate to one side and I can't grip it any-more and drop the bag in the dirt. So I lie down on the ground and try to roll the sandbag onto my torso because I can't pick it straight up and for some reason, I don't know why, I don't want to disappoint Joe. Then I spin the entire sandbag onto my chest and nearly crush myself. The ratio of this sandbag to

my weight is not proportional to the ratio of this sandbag to
Joe's or George's weight.

After a minute and a half of struggle and covering myself
in a fine layer of dirt, George comes over and puts the sandbag on my shoulders so I can walk twenty feet and drop it at
the top of the hill.

The sun is just rising, and everything is still and glistening in the mist. There's a little hut at the top of the hill out-
fitted with a cot and a furnace and a rock staircase Joe's been
working on. He hopes this'll become a Spartan training mecca
someday. He's put in fifty miles of trails all around here, he
says. Then he grabs a giant boulder.

"Fifty burpees," Joe orders. Then he disappears down the
other side of the hill while George and I bust out burpees.
Well, George does burpees, I do furpees. Faux burpees — burpees done on an incline to take some pressure off the shoulders.

Joe comes up the stairs at about the same time we finish
up our burpees and hands the boulder to George so he can do
a loop.

"Fifty burpees," Joe says. I start on my second set of burpees, Joe busting out his fifty by my side.

When George comes back up the hill, he's looking pretty
proud. That boulder probably weighs more than 180 pounds.
He tosses it onto the ground in a grand display of strength,
then the thing splits in two. Awkward silence.

"Well, I guess I showed that rock who's boss!" George says.
Joe doesn't reply.

Joe starts talking again once we begin our descent down the
other side of the hill.

Around Thanksgiving just after Joe was married, Joe's father had a heart attack. Joe and a buddy jumped into a Chevy Avalanche and bolted down Route 87 to go see Joe's dad in Queens. Joe's friend was driving eighty-five miles per hour when he fell asleep at the wheel, hit a tree, and spun the car around. Joe flew out of a window after whacking his knee on the glove compartment, sending his femur into his back.

Doctors told Joe they didn't know the extent of the damage to his hip. More specifically, they didn't know whether he'd ever be able to walk normally again. Then victims from another car crash were rolled into the hospital, and the doctors left Joe alone. So he pulled himself off the table and, after checking to make sure his friend was okay, wheeled himself out of there in his gown and hailed a taxi to take him from his hospital in Albany to his dad's in Queens. When he got there, he cleaned himself up and entered his dad's room.

His dad was fine, but Joe's injury was bad. Five doctors told him he was done. He'd never run again. No more competing. But one doctor at the Cornell Medical Center told him he had a chance. That he probably had six hours after the accident before his hip became necrotic and that he had lost maybe four hours between suffering the initial insult and undergoing surgery. But the doctor couldn't be sure how well Joe would recover. What he did know was that Joe couldn't pound his hip and that it would be helpful to get blood flowing to that area to assist the healing process.

So Joe went on an Ironman binge. Let's just do them all! he decided. He signed up for fifteen or sixteen Ironmans in one year. To train, he biked. And biked and biked and biked. And he did Pilates; yoga was off limits because he needed to tighten the muscles around his hip, not stretch them out. Joe's recovery plan must've worked, he figures, because he's been competing ever since.

A pine tree has fallen across the trail. George and Joe pick it up and move it like it's no big deal.

I ask Joe what he thinks of Tough Mudder. He gets this look in his eyes that I can't quite place. A little sad, mad. Devilish. Like a guy talking about an ex-girlfriend he hates but still thinks about a lot.

"It's bizarre that this Tough Mudder thing popped up on the Internet when we were launching," Joe says. "They wanted to meet with us, so we met with them. They wanted to use our Death Race as a comparison to Tough Mudder. We said no, they're not similar events in any stretch of the imagination. We thought Spartan Race would be a better comparison, but they didn't want to give Spartan Race any credit, so we didn't get anywhere. And then they started flying airplanes over our events. So we returned the favor."

It only got worse from there. "Then they started going after our venues and our race dates," Joe will tell me later.

As *Outside* magazine reported in an exposé of Will Dean's business tactics, Spartan Race hosted a successful event at Vail Lake Resort in Temecula, California, and renewed its contract for the next year. But before Joe announced his new race, Tough Mudder put a Vail Lake event on its calendar, scheduled for three weeks later.

"I tried to have a civil conversation [with Will Dean] about Temecula, and that's when it got insane," De Sena says. He got a call from an ex–Harvard professor who was advising Tough Mudder and who told him that if the two companies tried to change their event dates, "the government antitrust agency would come after me for collusion. I said, 'Do they teach in Harvard how to be dishonest and untruthful?' That's when I knew I was dealing with a screwball."

Dean sent Joe a fancy bottle of Scotch as a Christmas gift. "It was kind of tongue-in-cheek," Joe says.

When unusually muddy conditions forced Tough Mudder to cancel a race near Austin, Texas (it would've been too hard for medical crews to reach runners quickly), "we offered all of the people who felt cheated free entry to our race," which was nearby, Joe says. Then he got another Christmas gift: a copy of Dale Carnegie's *How to Win Friends and Influence People*. Inside, *Outside* magazine reported, was the following hand-written dedication:

"How nice of you to offer participants free entry. . . . No doubt a worthy strategy to focus on those customers who have not yet done the Mudder, for the likelihood of success with those who have would seem dim indeed." Signed, Will Dean.

Dean later claimed his chief marketing officer, Matthew Johnson, had written the note, which Johnson confirmed.

But Joe doesn't go into any of that right now while we're hiking. "It's been a very tumultuous relationship with them" is all he says, after mentioning the planes. "So we just avoid communication at this point."

We keep walking, the earth crunching beneath our feet. Then he adds, "One of the biggest things, for us, is for something to be an obstacle, it can't just hurt people. It can't be an electric shock—that's not an obstacle. It's gotta be athletic in nature."

We're almost back to Joe's house when George peels off to take a shower. Morning kung fu lessons have already begun in the big red barn. Joe drops the sandbag on his porch, revealing a tattoo on his inner left forearm in some sort of Eastern script, maybe Chinese. It's his mother's name.

"I didn't want to say anything in front of George, but I'm upset about that boulder," Joe says before heading inside. "I really liked that boulder."

There is someone in the inn. A young man, maybe seventeen years old, is sitting on the couch playing a video game called Skyrim. He's Tim, the innkeeper's son, and he's currently avoiding his sister's wedding activities.

I sit at a table behind him and ask if he's ever done a Spartan race, given that he lives in the birthplace of Spartan racing.

No, he says. He's going into the real military, so he doesn't do the races.

"Have you ever met Joe?"

"Joe seems like a nice guy from when I've met him. A lot of the local people don't like Joe. Jealousy, I guess," Tim says, eyes on the TV screen. "He employs a lot of the town, and the people who work for him love him."

I think about that sign in the general store—Joe's general store: LIVE SIMPLY . . . SO OTHERS CAN SIMPLY LIVE. Life can't be simple when you're responsible for practically an entire town's employment.

Tim flicks buttons on a remote, transforming his avatar into a werewolf so he can go on a nighttime killing rampage through a medieval castle. "Joe," Tim says as he slays an archer, "is the only reason there's any life in this town."

5

Throwing a CrossFit

ERIK TAYLOR IS a personal trainer who believes in the power of functional fitness to heal broken bodies and optimize health. He's a tall and handsome Shane West look-alike and a certified CrossFit coach, though he's never shelled out the $3,000 annual fee to associate his gym with the brand. He's also my neighbor, a few doors removed, and he's made it his personal mission to prepare me for the Ultra Beast.

I consider it pity training. Erik recently noticed me wogging around the block, wogging being a tedious activity in which an injured runner walks a minute, then jogs a minute, for ten minutes total, gradually expanding to twenty minutes. Someone in a forum dedicated to runners hobbled by enraged

Achilles tendons suggested doing it, so I decided to give it a try. Wogging is the only activity I think I can do without inducing shoulder, knee, or Achilles pain, and while it feels good to be doing *something*, my muscles, like houseplants, are shriveling up from relative neglect—the exact opposite training response I'd dreamed of when I signed up for the event.

After explaining to Erik what the Ultra Beast is (a marathon-distance obstacle race! on a ski mountain! I'm gonna die!), I must've seemed pretty pathetic because he offered to take on my case pro bono, though we'd never really spoken before. I was a fitness experiment he couldn't pass up.

Hypothesis: Erik can build an athlete from less than zero to Ultra Beast finisher in four weeks.

Method: Athlete will come to Erik's garage gym every day and do whatever Erik says for an hour while his three-year-old daughter, Mychaela, observes to ensure proper adherence to procedures as outlined on the whiteboard under the heading "The Erin Project." Athlete may wear whatever she wants, while Mychaela will dress only in Hello Kitty–issued shirts, skirts, shorts, pants, and shoes. Erik will email WODs on any day athlete is not in town. These WODs shall not be skipped, lest athlete choose to dig her own grave, which, actually, would make a great WOD.

Possible conflicts of interest: Athlete is a former triathlete with absolutely no formal strength training background whatsoever.

Results: TBD/pending.

Erik's gym looks like some sort of satellite training facility for the KGB, or at least how I'd picture one: sparse and utilitarian. Kettlebells, dumbbells, and weight plates line the walls of the two-car space. A few TRX straps—nylon bands marketed for fitness training—hang from the ceiling next to a pull-up bar. The only splurges are a cable pulley machine ("It's good for older and injured athletes," Erik says, almost apologizing for having a fancy piece of equipment) and industrial gray carpeting.

He starts me off doing exercises on the TRX so I can control how much pressure I put on my shoulder and on my knees. I do push-ups and rows and squats and lunges, with Erik correcting my form as I go.

Within about a week and a half, my pains start to fade, so Erik steps up the workouts. He shows me how to pick up a fifty-pound sandbag without hurting my back by hugging the weight close to my body. Then he sends me straight out in public, sandbag slung over my shoulder, to hike up and down the Avenue C staircase, a long, steep string of steps that leads down to the beach.

Shirtless people congregate there to show off their muscles as they run up and down the concrete. I'm not shirtless, but for the number of stares I get, I might as well be—except on Friday afternoons. That's when a group of at least twenty Herbalife supplement–sponsored athletes bust out an Avenue C WOD. They like my style. To them, I am "hardcore" rather than bonkers and deserve "mad respect" for hauling that sand up the stairs over and over again. When I tell an inquisitive Avenue C-er why I'm doing it, he says he wants to run an obstacle race too.

His goal makes me grin. This guy is living proof of a statement I'd just read somewhere: CrossFitters didn't know what they were training for until obstacle racing came along. But it's not a one-way relationship: the obstacle racing phenomenon could not have happened without CrossFit.

• • •

Flashback to 1995. Back then, gymnast and personal trainer Greg Glassman was getting kicked out of gym after gym for employing unconventional training methods. "He had clients race their way through repetitions on a weight machine, and at one facility he had them scramble up a 30-foot column in the middle of the room," an *Inc.* profile of Glassman states.

While gym owners didn't like his style, Glassman's SoCal clientele enjoyed his lifting- and sprint-based workouts. His routines combined the two holy Es craved by time-crunched, health-conscious people: efficiency and effectiveness.

At the time the sheriff's department in Santa Cruz, California, was also looking for a two-E training method. A friend who worked there asked Glassman to come coach the officers, and Glassman accepted the challenge. While he trained cops in a Santa Cruz gym, he refined his approach to developing full-body fitness.

"He liked the idea of throwing exercises at clients seemingly randomly, believing it resembled the way early humans had to overcome daily physical obstacles," *Inc.* says. Exercises should also target several muscle groups at once, Glassman believed, and be performed for time to discourage laziness. He would call his method CrossFit.

He developed a following fast. To keep up with demand, he started training people in pairs and quickly realized he was on to something. Not only did he make more money training two people at the same time, but they also enjoyed the workout more and pushed themselves harder.

"We all give more of ourselves in the presence of others—always, always," Glassman later told *Fast Company* magazine. "Performance goes up immediately." So he started adding more and more clients to each training session.

Eventually, he opened his own gym in a truck garage just

outside of town, all the while working to define his group-oriented creation. Everyone who came to his gym would perform the same workout together, he decided, with the workout altered only in load and intensity.

Glassman started posting a Workout of the Day, on Cross Fit.com in 2001 after his acolytes asked him to. They wanted to follow along when they were out of town. Little did Glassman know that by uploading those daily WODs, he had begun to lay the groundwork for two fitness empires.

CrossFit didn't exactly explode at first. In 2001, 80 percent of US Internet users had a dial-up connection, and Google had only just begun to revolutionize web search. But Glassman's online WODs proved highly addictive for those who found them, particularly when Glassman started naming the WODs after women.

Many early WODs got monikers like Angie, Chelsea, Barbara, and Fran. According to CrossFit lore, Glassman once explained the lady names like this: "Any workout that leaves you flat on your back, staring up at the sky, wondering what the hell happened, deserves a girl's name."

In 2005 Glassman also started naming WODs after fallen service members—soldiers and police officers killed in the line of duty. It was a nod to CrossFit's growing popularity in the American military and police academies. Murph, for example, was named after Navy Lieutenant Michael Murphy, an avid CrossFitter who was killed in Afghanistan. The workout, a one-mile run followed by 100 pull-ups, 200 push-ups, 300 squats, and a final one-mile run was one of the twenty-nine-year-old's favorites.

Murphy wasn't just one of a few soldiers who embraced Glassman's high-intensity regimen. Entire military branches—

the Army Rangers and the Marine Corps in particular—were anxious to revamp their training programs with workouts better geared toward combat readiness.

"In recent decades we have not maintained our focus on combat when we designed our physical fitness programs," wrote Lieutenant General James F. Amos in a paper on Marine Corps fitness, referring to the traditional endurance routines the Marines had been doing.* "Our physical training was not 'functional' in this sense." But CrossFit training was.

Marines and members of every other US military branch began CrossFitting. By 2006, Glassman estimated, nearly 7,000 US soldiers were regularly following his program.

Thousands of civilians were also getting hooked on Cross-Fit, thanks to Glassman's decision to start an affiliate program. Glassman refused to call his business model "franchising." Franchises, to him, were strictly regulated and bottom-line-oriented. Glassman's attitude was much more laissez-faire and altruistic—somewhat reminiscent of Mr. Mouse's corporate philosophy.

"I have a real problem with any business activity that isn't about value creation," Glassman once said. "Money is essential to run a business, but it's not why you run a business. It is not what makes business grow. Businesses grow on dreams. Trying to make money is no way to run a business."

Glassman gave athletes and entrepreneurs permission to develop their own versions of his Santa Cruz "box" (the CrossFit term for a gym) and stamp them with the CrossFit name. Box owners simply had to attend a certification semi-

---

* "A Concept for Functional Fitness," US Marine Corps Combat Development Command, November 9, 2006.

nar and pay an annual affiliation fee; then they were free to do as they pleased with both their business and their workouts.

CrossFit North in Seattle was the first box to affiliate, and a dozen more all over the United States quickly followed. Over the next few years the number of US CrossFit boxes would grow to more than a thousand, thanks to the eruption of social media.

Glassman was a social media master before there was Web 2.0—before businesses were buzzing about search engine optimization and user engagement, page views and click-through rates. Social media was a new way to link individuals together and build a sense of community, something at which Glassman had already proven himself adept.

In the early 2000s, Glassman took to blogging easily. He started CrossFit Journal, a blog he used to preach the CrossFit gospel to the web-connected masses. He wrote about transforming garages into simple but effective gyms and about goal setting. He philosophized about fitness, arguing, for example, that because decathlete Simon Poelman crushes six-time Ironman winner and "fittest man on earth" Mark Allen in all measures of strength, power, speed, and coordination, Poelman is the earth's true fittest guy.

Glassman's open-source business attitude carried into his online life. He welcomed guest bloggers and invited people to interact with the WODs by posting their times in the comments.

As more and more social media sites popped up—Facebook in 2004, YouTube in 2005, Twitter in 2006—more and more people posted status updates and videos and photos of themselves performing WODs, inventing WODs, asking for tips on form and box design, and asking how to affiliate. Hun-

dreds of thousands of people wanted to be a part of Glassman's community-oriented fitness brand. As more and more
people joined social media sites that number would quickly
climb into the millions.

It's not hard to understand their fervor; it was a reaction to
living in a culture that was becoming increasingly isolating.

"We already emphasized individuals," says University of
Colorado sociologist Jay Coakley. "But we have taken that to
an extreme. We moved toward this individual model where
everybody's responsible for themselves, and away from community sponsorship."

Glassman seemed to inherently understand that issue.
And to realize that the new way Americans sought to cultivate
community—through social media—could also be isolating.
He knew CrossFit was uniquely poised to take advantage of
America's search for community both online and off. Unlike
many other groups grown through social media, CrossFitters
had somewhere to go every day—boxes all across the country
where they could see each other face to face.

That combination of Internet and in-person community was intoxicating, and it helped CrossFit's popularity sky-
rocket. As social networking sites grew, so did CrossFit. By
the time Instagram launched in 2010, CrossFit boasted almost
1,700 affiliates and 58 nonprofit military affiliates throughout
the world.

The activity's mushrooming success earned Glassman a
nickname of his own: The WODfather. And just like Cor-
leone, this Don did not rise to the top of his game without
controversy.

Perhaps the first big CrossFit scandal occurred when the *New
York Times* ran a story about the potential negative side ef-

fects of Glassman's high-intensity, heavily weighted workouts. Titled "Getting Fit, Even If It Kills You," the article outlined a rare but potentially fatal side effect of lifting too much too fast: rhabdomyolysis, a breakdown of muscle fibers in which muscle proteins are leaked into the bloodstream and poison the kidneys.

In response to the *Times* reporter's questions about Cross-Fit's risks, Glassman made a few now-infamous statements: "It can kill you. I've always been completely honest about that," he said. "If you find the notion of falling off the rings and breaking your neck so foreign to you, then we don't want you in our ranks."

Not only that, the *Times* article revealed a few things about CrossFit culture that shocked nonfollowers. "An axiom among practitioners," the article read, "is 'I met Pukey,' meaning they worked out so hard they vomited. Some even own T-shirts emblazoned with a clown, Pukey. CrossFit's other mascot is Unkle Rhabdo, another clown, whose kidneys have spilled onto the floor presumably due to rhabdomyolysis."

Later, Glassman would write a comment on his own website that flaunted CrossFit's frat guy humor and nut-up attitude. "We have a therapy for injuries at CrossFit called STFU," he typed. STFU meaning Shut the F— Up.

Glassman didn't know it, but everything he'd done since posting that first WOD online set the scene for OCR's explosive growth. He mapped out a way to unite people, both online and off, through a fitness brand. And he created a culture of peer-pressure-induced athletic achievement that OCR would happily adopt.

In an interview with *New York Business Journal*, Will Dean would echo Glassman's "it can kill you" speech when he de-

clared that Tough Mudder wasn't for everyone. "If you're unsure," Dean said, "you shouldn't do it."

Tough Mudder would employ the same sort of frater-
nity culture in all of its branding, from obstacle descriptions
("Dong Dingler: Mudders must cross a body of water with
just one slippery rope to hold on to. Forget about trying to
keep your jewels warm, just suck it up and Mudder on") to
on-course signage (WIMPS GO THIS WAY, TOUGH MUDDERS
GO THAT WAY).

Spartan Race would send out daily Spartan-branded
WODs and design its obstacles to reward athletes with all-
around strength.

In that same *New York Business Journal* interview, Dean
would even credit CrossFit—without naming it—and its
blend of social media and in-person contact for the success
of OCR.

But the biggest contributor to OCR's success was the Cross-
Fit community itself. By 2010, Greg Glassman had assembled
an international army of team-oriented athletes ready for combat with nowhere to go—gobs of people who didn't know what
they were training for until obstacle racing came along.

From 2010 on, OCR would blast off side by side with
CrossFit, each fueling the other's growth. Eventually, CrossFit
would even share its title sponsor, Reebok, with Spartan Race.

"A lot of the time you're in the gym and you're like, 'Wow,
a period of my life is now dedicated to squatting and push-
ups,'" says Dogtown CrossFit owner Dusty Hyland. "You
want to get back out and live life a little bit too."*

* In 2007, Glassman launched the CrossFit games, a WOD-based competition
designed to find the Fittest on Earth. "At the end of the day, it's very much an
individual sport when you're trying to find the fittest man and woman on the

REDONDO BEACH, CALIFORNIA
T-3.5 WEEKS UNTIL THE ULTRA BEAST

Back in my trainer-neighbor's box, Erik Taylor says he has reservations about CrossFit. While he likes the high-intensity, strength-based regimen, he does not like the community aspect. Erik likes to tailor workouts (no pun intended) to an athlete's specific goals. Workouts performed at random, he says, may make people perennially "combat ready," but not likely PR (personal-record) ready.

My own CrossFit reservations come from the lack of cardio. I have no idea how I'm doing with this functional fitness training; my internal fit-meter only reads high-volume cardio. For almost a decade, I could tell that I was getting better at something because I could go longer. I could run one more mile than the week before, swim more, bike faster. With circuit training, I don't know how to gauge my progress, and it's driving me nuts. I have to blindly trust that Erik can see improvement. That when he says he thinks I can do the Ultra Beast after a month of swinging kettlebells and hiking stairs, he means it. I just don't believe him.

Even hard-core CrossFitters will admit that it's tough to run a marathon on CrossFit alone. Those who want to race endurance events usually supplement their training, adding mileage under the guidance of a super-controversial powerlifting ultrarunner named Brian MacKenzie.

Brian MacKenzie, or BMac, as his disciples often call him, is the founder of CrossFit Endurance, a splinter group of the

---

planet," Hyland says. OCR caters better to the greater CrossFit community of people who enjoy working out together.

CrossFit movement whose popularity lies in one single promise: you can compete in ultradistance events on only six to eight hours of training per week. Marathons, ultramarathons, Ironmans—you name it, you can do it on a CrossFit Endurance regimen.

It's a promise that captivates day-job-riddled athletes, and one that sent the running world up in arms. BMac's been bashed in every endurance forum on the Internet. "What a complete f'n tool." "MacKenzie is a whack-job who talks a much bigger game than he plays." MacKenzie has the word UNSCARED tattooed across his knuckles, Reverend Harry Powell style, which doesn't help his cause among elite runners either.*

The issue comes down to science. Can short, high-intensity exercise induce the same physiological changes as logging the long miles prescribed in traditional marathon plans? It's a tricky question to answer because there's still some debate as to which physiological changes are most responsible for getting runners across a marathon finish line.

BMac latches on to the measurement of VO_2 max, the maximum amount of oxygen a person can use during intense exercise. The higher your VO_2 max, the better you'll be at endurance exercise, it's been thought, and short, high-intensity training has been shown to improve VO_2 max better than long, slow distance.†

But several studies have demonstrated that improvement in running performance, like being able to run faster and longer,

---

* Their tattoo of choice: the winged foot of Mercury, messenger to the gods.
† To read an abstract of the study (J. Helgerud et al., "Aerobic High-Intensity Intervals Improve VO_2 max More Than Moderate Training," *Medicine and Science in Sports and Exercise* [April 2007]), go to: http://www.ncbi.nlm.nih.gov/pubmed/17414804.

may not have much to do with aerobic changes. Instead, researchers have found that gradually building up mileage and running long distances, as a traditional marathon training plan advises, creates important muscular adaptations that allow people to tackle the race more efficiently. Muscles get smaller, but they contract faster and use less oxygen to go the same speed. Power output also increases. These changes, running coaches argue, are absolutely necessary if you want to run your best marathon. CrossFit Endurance, by contrast, promises a good marathon on weekly mileage of ten miles or less.

Several athletes, broken and not, have turned to BMac with an almost cultlike religious fervor. They want to sign up for their favorite race and compete without logging long miles. They believe in his method because they want to believe that it will work. That way, they're not completely out of the game because they're injured, or because they started a family, or because they work long hours.

And now I'm in Erik's gym for much the same reason. I want to believe that I can finish the Ultra Beast without much running—or with no running at all, really. But I don't.

Erik apparently has prepared a pep talk to counter my can't-do attitude. The Ultra Beast is not a traditional marathon, he says. For the obstacle race, functional strength training is essential. Sure, if I could run, I'd finish faster. But the real key to finishing that kind of event is strength. Strength and mental fortitude.

Erik's job is to address the imbalances and strength issues that are exacerbating my injuries and to make me as buff as possible in four weeks. Because more than cardiovascular endurance, I will need strong muscles to scramble up ropes and over walls and to do burpees. My job is to visualize myself conquering the race, quit pouting about my rogue Achilles, and

get my game face on. In other words, SUCK IT UP AND
PULL IT TOGETHER!

I drink Erik's Kool-Aid because I have to. But it doesn't
take long until I start to believe in his methods. After a few
weeks of daily visits to Erik's garage, I get addicted to his
WODs. Each new workout written under "The Erin Project"
on the whiteboard promises to bring me closer to Beast mode,
and knowing that makes me feel all warm and fuzzy inside.
The routine is not only beefing up my quads, it's also repairing my athletic confidence.

That is why, when Erik cancels a workout on me days before the Ultra Beast,* I have a mini-meltdown.

And that is the evening Jimmy brings home two twenty-
pound bags of kitty litter.

"Think you got enough kitty litter?" I ask. We have a cat,
but Sir Galahad is not that crappy.

"Change into your workout clothes," Jimmy says.

"What are we doing?"

"You'll see."

I slip on some spandex and follow Jimmy to the yard.

"Grab a bag," Jimmy says.

"Of kitty litter?"

"Yes."

"Why?"

"Just grab it," Jimmy says.

"What am I going to do with it?"

"Stop asking so many questions!"

"This situation warrants questions!"

"Just pick it up, please." My triathlon coach, it appears,

---

* My Hello Kitty workout partner knocked out her entire family with a pre-
school virus after only one day in class.

is improvising. Last weekend, fearing for my endurance, he made me march twelve miles around the neighborhood with him after drenching myself in an outdoor shower. He called it the Wet Seal WOD. Now there's this.

Kitty litter crunching on our backs, we walk down the Strand, the bike path that lines the beaches of Los Angeles. People are playing volleyball and jogging and cycling, and all of those people are staring at us, the neighborhood nuts. One woman restrains her tiny dog, who is clearly turned on by the smell of Tidy Cats.

Jimmy marches straight up the Avenue C stairs, and I follow. When we walk by Erik's house, I pray he doesn't see us.

We drop our kitty litter bags in the yard. Jimmy hesitates for a second, like he wants to put them inside.

"No one's gonna steal our kitty litter," I say. "Now what?"

"Now we wog the same loop, then do it all again two more times."

"I'm telling Erik you made me carry kitty litter all over the place," I say as we start walking. I can't believe this is one of my last workouts before heading to Vermont. "I shall call this WOD Pooper Scooper."

5.5

Training Day

KILLINGTON, VERMONT

SEPTEMBER 20, TWO DAYS BEFORE THE ULTRA BEAST
1900-ish

VERMONT'S ROUTE 4 is postcard romantic. White build-ings and barns glow in the twilight. A pale rainbow of red, orange, and yellow leaves swirls in the snappy September air. While Jimmy drives, I pretend we're tourists on a relaxing date weekend, sipping maple lattes, waiting for the first ruby-red leaves to show. But the honeymoon ends when we pull up to the Killington Grand Hotel and I see race supplies tossed across the ski slopes. That makes me want to barf.

The Ultra Beast anticipation wouldn't be so nerve-racking if I knew I wouldn't be facing it alone. But Robyn, my part-ner in endurance crime, is not coming. She had a disastrous lead-up to what was supposed to be her fourth iron-distance triathlon. First, she got strep throat. Then a bee stung her just under the eye while she was on a training ride, and her face puffed up like someone punched her. Then she got a reaction to the medication for the strep throat and got all itchy when she worked out. Then she got a kidney stone. A pretty good-sized one. To get rid of it, her doctor told her, she had to pass it. She was still working on that when Jimmy and I left for Vermont. It looks like it's just going to be me and that mountain on race day.

The hotel is at the base of the ski slopes, across a pond from the lifts and the start of the Ultra Beast. Tents are already set up, and other equipment is lying around. Somewhere out there are 2,100 feet of barbed wire, 250 sandbags, 150 bales of hay, three cords of firewood, and 115 spears. All in all, there are 120 tons of material scattered about that dark forest, waiting to maim and torture me and Jimmy and 4,228 other people nutty enough to sign up for this weekend's races.

I figure I have forty or so hours to live. That gives me a good four hours on course before I perish, fading into a vague, misty blackness while Jimmy whispers into the wind the most well deserved "I told you so!" in endurance sports history.

KILLINGTON, VERMONT
SEPTEMBER 21, ONE DAY BEFORE THE ULTRA BEAST
1530-ish

I spend my last morning on earth searching for electrolytes. It's been so long since I last raced, I forgot to bring the one thing that'll help keep my body, including my heart, functioning properly. So Jimmy and I set out on a mission to get some. SaltStick capsules. Electrolyte chews. I don't care what we find. There are several ski shops in town, open and ready to take advantage of the estimated 8,000 people the Spartan race is bringing into the area this weekend, but none of them has electrolyte supplements.

One store is selling soap etched with Margaret's DIRT IN YOUR SKIRT logo. Another has T-shirts picturing a bear with antlers and saying BEER under the mutant creature. All of the stores have enormous animals fashioned out of straw outside their doors. I've seen a straw Dalmatian, bear, moose, cow, and pig, and even a straw frog prince. But no electrolytes. None whatsoever. After visiting three ski shops and the grocery store, we give up and decide to get our race packets.

Almost everyone in the big white packet-pickup tent is wearing black Spartan shirts. Those who aren't look somewhat out of place, like Bambi hanging out in a pack of pumas. A Jason Mraz look-alike is playing guitar and singing so loud it's hard to think. I wonder if Joe De Sena instructed the guy to do that on purpose just to see who would quit now, unable to weather the amplified crooning long enough to flash an ID and grab a race bib.

Looking around, it's clear that Jimmy and I are not in triathlonland anymore. To start, there are noticeably more tattoos. Triathletes who have tattoos generally only have one, in the shape of an M-dot (the Ironman logo), positioned on the backs of their calves to let people cycling or running behind them know that they've covered 140.6 miles in one day.

Those M-dotted triathletes are also often lean and totally hairless. A lot of the men in this noisy tent are furry and totally stacked. So when a baby-faced, bespectacled man approaches Jimmy and me as we stand in line, I figure it's to form an alliance, a fellow Spartan newbie trying not to psych himself out in a sea of facial hair. I figure wrong.

The forty-year-old is a fellow Ultra Beast hopeful who goes by the name Matt B. Davis. A Warrior Dash tipped him head-over-heels in love with obstacle racing a few years ago, he says, so much so that he started a podcast about the sport. He's dropped fifteen pounds since he started competing, and he knows everyone who's anyone in the OCR world. Like this guy over here. Yeah, that one with the black Team SISU T-shirt. We gotta meet Daren de Heras! He's a bona fide obstacle racer who lives and trains in Southern California, just like me and Jimmy!

If I'd had any idea at that moment what a bona fide obstacle racer's Ultra Beast training was like, I'd have driven straight down the ski mountain and hightailed it back to LA.

Team SISU Workout

SEAL BEACH, CALIFORNIA
AUGUST 31
0800

You will need: two five-gallon buckets, a bike, and a sledgehammer or maul. That's what the Facebook event post says. Also, enough fuel for six hours of hard labor. Meet at 0800 where First Street hits Southern California's Seal Beach. If you see a parking lot and the River's End Café, you're in the right place.

To the uninitiated, it would seem like the Mafia is recruiting soldiers through social media for a massive operation. But the twenty-three people who show up are soldiers of a different kind. They're members of Team SISU, the extreme training branch of the Weeple Army, which at the moment is the largest OCR team in the country at more than 1,300 strong.*

SISU (*see-sue*) is named after a Thor-like, twenty-eight-pound "war hammer" sold online for $125. *Sisu* means "stubborn determination" in Finnish. Also: spunk, guts, grit, perseverance, pluck, and balls.†

Daren de Heras created this elite team with one overarching goal: to forge unbreakable athletes. But to do that, he apparently has to destroy them first.

It's already 80 degrees outside when the trainees show up. These men and women, ranging in age from their twenties to their sixties, include bus drivers and businesspeople, Marines and Army parachutists. A few kids for heckling and extra weight.

They're all wearing either a black SISU T-shirt or a neon-green Weeple Army shirt. Except for the guy with no shirt. Patrick Scully sports only tiny spandex shorts, a necklace, and a half-ponytail. He looks like Conan the Barbarian, tanned, toned muscles glistening in the sun. The women dining at the River's End Café take notice and move tables closer to the sand.

Daren and his partner-in-pain, Matt Trinca, kick off the

---

* The Weeples are named after none other than those little fluffy, armless give-away toys popular in the '80s and '90s, which, incidentally, made a recent come-back in the Netherlands thanks to a supermarket's FIFA World Cup promotion, no thanks to OCR.

† Perhaps needed to hawk a heavy stick for $125.

day's exercises by ordering everyone to haul massive truck tires, as well as their buckets and mauls, out to the beach from a cargo truck dubbed "the Death Van."

"Not tired!" Scully yells. Then he drops a twenty-five-pound sledgehammer in the sand and joins the group as they form a giant circle around de Heras and Trinca.

Everybody loosens up with fifty jumping jacks, six squats, sun salutations, hip openers, and worm walks. Just enough movement to work up a sweat. Then the real workout starts.

The beach portion of today's torture will be a medley of WODs. But these guys aren't tackling just one WOD—they're pounding out four, back to back. And before Team SISU can start on those, they must complete a task.

De Heras and Trinca split everyone into groups of six, then draw parallel lines in the sand about ten feet apart. The first team to run to the other side, assemble in a human pyramid, and hold that position for ten seconds wins the challenge and is immune from penalty.

After the winning structure disassembles, Trinca fans out four sealed envelopes that read "funishment." A representative of the losing teams picks one and tears it open. The funishment: buddy-carry, 200 yards out across the sand, 200 yards back. This is where it starts to get interesting.

Everybody—including the winning team—buddies up, and each pair takes off, one guy running, the other slung over his shoulder or riding piggyback. And when they return, quads, shoulders, backs, and biceps on fire, de Heras tells them to do it again. No complaints. Everybody throws on a human weight vest and trudges through the sand, again. These guys are clearly gluttons for pain. Double-buddy-carry complete, it's time to tackle the WODs.

First up: the SISU Century. That's twenty burpees, a sadistic but effective exercise combining a push-up with a jump into the air; follow that up with twenty squats while holding a maul or sledgehammer overhead; twenty alternating jump split squats; twenty V-ups; and twenty push-ups.

"Name your maul!" de Heras shouts.

"Not Tired!" Scully shouts back, squatting deep, clutching his twenty-five-pound neon-green weapon of destruction overhead.

Once that's done, it's straight into WOD number two, a six-leg relay race broken up as follows: carry two buckets filled with sand 200 meters, then sprint 200 meters; sprint 200 meters, then carry one bucket filled with sand in front of your chest; carry three tires 400 meters; sprint 200 meters, then do 200 meters of burpee broad jumps (a burpee followed by a two-legged leap forward); 200 meters of cartwheels, then a 200-meter sprint; and a 200-meter log roll, followed by a 200-meter sprint.

After each team member picks which leg he will complete—according to perceived strengths and puke-proofness—the race is on. Scully makes a spectacular show of his burpee broad jumps, practically bouncing into his push-ups, then letting out a war cry as he shoots forward, much to the amusement of his growing fan club.

Another SISU team member who goes by Cookie says that one day he decided to do an entire set of burpee broad jumps straight through Long Beach. It took him three hours and laid him out for two solid days afterward. Totally worth it, he says, and totally not doing that again without a really good reason. This team relay is not a really good enough reason. He carries three tires, one around his neck, one in each hand.

The losing teams' funishment this time: a 400-meter bear crawl—a walk on all fours—through the sand, naturally. Everybody jumps in, naturally. "Butts down!" de Heras barks. For SISU members with bad wrists, he allows the use of forearms, as well as crab walking. By the last 100 meters, there's a large contingent of baby crawlers, but de Heras lets it slide. It's time for WOD number three, a group exercise that proves to be the highlight of the show.

The sun comes out in full force to illuminate Scully's eight-pack as he and everyone else wield their mauls and hammers and pound fifty overhead strikes into the sand. New onlookers are likely thinking they've stumbled upon either a mass grave digging or a prison workout. Either way, they look a bit bug-eyed.

Next up: partner drills. One partner lies on the ground and raises his or her legs, while the other one tries to throw the supine partner's legs back at the sand. Then they each do ten handstand push-ups and twenty seated dips with the buckets. Finally, everyone planks in a circle. Front planks, side planks, back bridges. Just when de Heras and Trinca believe everyone is satisfactorily destroyed, they announce WOD number four: tug-of-war.

Biceps curl, feet struggle to dig into the sand, and the teams heave and ho until all but one have toppled. It's time for the final funishment, tentatively drawn from Trinca's sandy hands. The envelope is slowly peeled open and a piece of paper unfolded. "Run to the ocean, and fully submerge," it reads.

It's understandable why nobody hesitates to take this funishment. It's noon, it's sunny, it's over 80 degrees—and they're only halfway done.

. . .

Team SISU members pack their buckets, mauls, hammers, and tires back into the Death Van, then bust out bikes. They're going to ride twenty-five miles straight inland from the beach along the San Gabriel River path. Inland means hotter. It also means riding through some notoriously sketchy neighborhoods just east of Compton where other cyclists have fought off hooded shotgun-wielding thugs.

Luckily, the only guys out on the river path looking to break Team SISU are de Heras and Trinca. They set a respectable though not terribly difficult pace of thirteen miles per hour, letting the thick heat inflict pain instead of the speed.

It must be 100 degrees when everyone hits the halfway point. There, in a tiny patch of shade on the side of a dried-up canal, it would appear that the training overlords stopped to let the team refuel. In reality, it's time for a challenge.

"Grab your bikes!" de Heras says. Then he points to the 45-degree concrete canal wall to the left of the bike path. Anyone who can carry his bike up and down the wall at least five times will get five seconds off of his obstacle course time, Trinca says. Each extra trip beyond that gets you an extra second off—and you really want seconds off. There's a $35 REI gift card and mountains of pride at stake.

Right now, most athletes would be praying their bikes were featherlight carbon fiber and muttering obscenities to themselves. It's not an uncommon reaction when you have a set vision for a workout, like riding twenty-five miles, and then your coach throws a mean curveball. But Team SISU doesn't have that attitude. They hoist their beach cruisers and full-suspension mountain bikes onto their backs and start marching up and down the wall. With so much gusto even that Trinca has to limit the maximum number of earned seconds off to ten. It's almost shocking that none of them actually says, "Thank you, sir, may I have another?" But maybe not surprising considering there's a Marine and a former Army lieutenant who's jumped out of a plane 282 times in the mix.

The team is only one mile from the end of the ride when someone finally drops. Amber, de Heras's girlfriend, has heat exhaustion, and she has it bad. Goose bumps, weakness, the whole bit. Each team member signed a waiver this morning absolving Team SISU of any liability in the event of "heat prostration," but it certainly won't release de Heras from future girlfriend retaliation.*

The team members cool her down with ice bags from a nearby gas station, then make their way to the final challenge: the Rio Hondo Police Academy obstacle course.

At this point, SISU has been working out for more than eight hours. But they can't go home until they complete one final task: a timed run through the obstacle course.

It's simple-looking enough. Scale a chain-link fence, then a wooden wall, crawl through a drainpipe, swing across monkey bars, jump over a wood bar, tiptoe across a balance beam, jump over a brick wall, zigzag through some thigh-high bars, then sprint a lap around a track, and finito, you're done!

"Not tired!" Scully yells after he crushes the course. He runs after everyone else, screaming encouragement, filming their efforts until his phone dies.

It's 6:00 PM when everyone has a course time—ten hours

_____

* Jimmy would know. When we were dating, he took me on a hot, treacherous, fourteen-mile trail run in the Santa Monica Mountains. Except he ran far ahead of me and didn't mark the trail. All I could think about as I stumbled down the dirt was how hard I was gonna kick him in the pants when I found him.

after Team SISU started in Seal Beach. A car parked nearby to shuttle the athletes back to the ocean reads 101 on its rearview mirror temperature gauge.

That's how elite obstacle racers spend a Saturday. Says de Heras, "Wait till you see what we're doing tomorrow."

Back under the Ultra Beast packet-pickup tent, ignorance is truly bliss. If I were to size up de Heras right now, I'd say he looks like any other fit thirty-nine-year-old. About my height, five-foot-seven. Toned arms and chest puffing out his Team SISU tee. I know nothing about his training techniques. I don't know that twenty times up the Avenue C stairs would be a warm-up for him, or that he'll do four WODs in a row and then some. But I'm about to learn something about his obstacle racing résumé.

De Heras tells me and Jimmy that he completed the Death Race. It took him sixty-two and a half hours—more than two and a half days straight, with no sleep. He was in a wheelchair for a week afterward because he was so messed up he couldn't walk. De Heras had blisters and a bacterial infection in his feet, a severe electrolyte imbalance that weakened his right hip, and a broken big toe.

Jimmy's jaw practically unhinges. He's never seen any reason to race longer than four hours, maybe five. There are plenty of challenging things to do in that time range, because going faster is hard, Jimmy always says whenever I try to get him to do something big with me. Going longer is less of an athletic challenge and more of a mental crusade.

It looks like Jimmy's about to say something, maybe to that effect, so I discreetly shake my head. Sharing that philosophy in this crowd could result in a mauling or hammering.

Besides, de Heras's wild story is about to get even crazier: he blames his Death Race–mangled body on Tough Mudder.

On April 7, 2011, at 9:15 AM, Tough Mudder posted a Facebook update that simultaneously delighted and bewildered the Mudder community. It said:

> We officially announce the 2011 World's Toughest Mudder, to be held Dec. 17–18, 2011 at the infamous Raceway Park, New Jersey. For 24 hrs, competitors will run non-stop loops of the Toughest Event on the Planet. The winner = the World's Toughest Mudder. Interested? Finish top 5% of your Mudder Class (and get therapy).

The announcement quickly garnered more than 100 comments, largely enthusiastic, with no fewer than two references to World's Toughest Mudder–induced boners. But the new event also threw dedicated Mudders into a philosophical conundrum: wasn't the point of Tough Mudder—the entire Tough Mudder culture—based on camaraderie? Wasn't it a "leave no man behind," "help thy neighbor," untimed team event? Mudders had always understood that Tough Mudder was not a race, but a challenge, one that put teamwork and camaraderie before individual course time. Why create a race?

Part of it had to do with the "probably." *Probably* the toughest event on the planet. That was Tough Mudder's tagline. "Probably," it seemed, just wasn't good enough for Will Dean. Not as long as Joe De Sena had *the* toughest obstacle event on earth in the Death Race. Tough Mudder's announcement was akin to a declaration of war on the Spartan empire—with the title of Toughest at stake.

But taking down De Sena's beloved Death Race was not the only incentive to create World's Toughest Mudder. Another reason stemmed from a simple truth spoken by General George Patton in 1944: Americans love a winner.

In the beginning, Tough Mudder had huge success marketing itself as a team event and rolling out a shock-and-awe campaign spearheaded by its Electroshock Therapy obstacle. But De Sena was busy building a weapon poised to steal away headlines and hearts, a weapon Will Dean could not possibly have without timed results: a winner.

His name is Hobie Call.

6

Hobie Call and the $100,000 Prize

IN THE OBSTACLE racing world, Hobie is a giant, the sport's first legend. In his kitchen in Erda, Utah, the wiry thirty-five-year-old stands about five-foot-eight, eyes twinkling through rimless oval glasses.

This is the man everyone wants to meet, a headline writer's dream. "Air Conditioning Repairman Unstoppable!" "Father of Five Dominates Grueling Race!"

Holbrook "Hobie" Call certainly didn't believe he'd become a sports icon in his midthirties; he has a wife and five kids between the ages of three and thirteen to support. But he could never shake his dream of becoming a professional athlete. That dream gripped his heart at age ten and never let go.

It wasn't just some wild boyhood fantasy either. Hobie really had talent. When he was nine, he entered his first marathon in St. George, Utah, then dropped out after nine miles because the media attention was too much for him to handle.

Everybody wanted to talk to the little prodigy, the sixth of ten kids from Star Valley, Wyoming, whose dad had once clocked a 2:34 marathon. But Hobie was chronically shy. He tried to run the marathon again when he was thirteen, but dropped out with a hip injury.

At fifteen, he decided to bike more than two hundred miles from his father's place in Provo to his mother's home in Star Valley, Wyoming. It took him a day, and later on, his twelve-year-old brother, Forest, rode all the way back with him. That's how Hobie did things growing up—going on grand adventures and playing outside.

He excelled at running in high school. As one reporter tells it, Hobie won his high school meets by such a wide margin that he had more than enough time to flip around and cross the finish line backward. Competition brought a showboater out from behind that reserved exterior.

Hobie went on to earn a scholarship to the College of Southern Idaho, where he was an All-American in track and cross-country, which was nice and all. But most important, he got to train with a raven-haired beauty one year above him who was also attending college on a running scholarship. Her name was Irene, and she was fast, and somewhere in between preseason running camp and two-a-day practices they started to fall for each other.

Irene liked Hobie's laugh and upbeat attitude. It was hard to get to know him, though, because of his shyness. But Hobie made sure Irene would never forget him when the two entered a boxing ring together to spar for some extra cash and Hobie accidentally clocked Irene right in the jaw. She couldn't open her mouth for a week.

Irene wasn't angry about it, though. She knew what she had with Hobie was love. Caveman-slug-woman-take-her-home-style love, perhaps, but love nonetheless. Hobie proposed, and the two were married while they were still in college.

But while all was relatively good in the relationship department, all was not good with Hobie's running coach, whose wooden training philosophy did not gel with the fun-loving Mr. Call.

Hobie liked dodging into ravines and turning a run into an excuse to explore off the beaten path. His coach enjoyed enforcing strict two-a-day workouts that were wearing Hobie down, constantly leaving him on the brink of injury. Hobie felt anxious all of the time just waiting to see what his coach would throw at him next. Finally, he couldn't take it anymore. Just two months before graduation, Hobie quit the team. He lost his scholarship and did not finish college. Hobie has had to do manual labor ever since.

"That's why we always tell the kids to stay in school!" Irene says. Heavy lifting was a tough gig for someone who still had his heart set on making the Olympic marathon team, a goal for which Hobie and his family would give—and lose—everything.

After college, Hobie worked odd jobs here and there. He did construction in Jackson, Wyoming. He worked in a specialty candy shop making caramels and popcorn and jams, always outproducing his fellow candy makers by at least 100 percent, as he remembers.

Finally, he and Irene settled in La Verkin, a small town just outside of St. George, Utah, where Hobie spent four and a half years working as a counselor at Cross Creek, a boarding school for troubled teens and at-risk youth. He credits that job with cracking his shyness shell; it's tough keeping young boys in line without exuding authority.

Throughout all of the moves and jobs, Hobie trained—he gets cranky when he doesn't exercise, Irene says. And he patiently waited for that one moment when those long hours of running would pay off and he could fulfill his boyhood dream of becoming a professional athlete.

Finally, in 2007, Hobie decided it was time to try to make the Olympic marathon team. He had prepared very seriously for a year, and it looked like all of the training and sacrifice would pay off when he ran a 2:16:38 at the Top of Utah marathon—fast enough to qualify for the 2008 US Olympic marathon trials in New York City. Hobie knew that if he was going to go for it, it was now or never.

At that point, Hobie had been working as a gym custodian, so he and Irene decided to take out a $50,000 second mortgage on their home to allow Hobie to train full-time for the trials for three months, no extra energy-sapping manual labor required. He had to buckle down and prepare for his one big chance to make it as an elite endurance athlete.

He followed a typical marathon program, running about ninety miles a week spread across speed workouts, tempo, and endurance runs, gradually winding down the weeks before the big race.

On November 3, 2007, he'd compete on the biggest running stage in the country in front of agents and sponsors and his wife and kids. He had a shot at becoming an Olympian and being invited to run for Nike or Brooks like the big shots he would compete against. His dream was coming true.

When the time came to fly to New York, he kissed the kids good-bye, packed up his running gear, and prayed that November 3 would be his lucky day.

But Hobie didn't feel right from the start. His legs felt heavy, like they wouldn't go any faster. And they *had* to go faster. His body was slowing down, and there was nothing he could do about it. He thought he might have food poisoning. The only time he'd ever felt like that before, food poisoning was to blame. Come on, body! This can't be happening . . . not now! Can't. Keep. Going . . .

So this was it. The moment when everything Hobie had dreamed of, sacrificed for, had arrived, and now something he'd eaten—he didn't know what—was making it impossible for him to run. He dropped out of the race about halfway through, utterly defeated. The next day he felt fine, physically.

At home, however, he was depressed. So depressed he couldn't get out of bed. He wouldn't leave his room for two weeks, Irene says. And just when it seemed nothing could get any worse, the US housing market began to slide. The Calls quickly owed more money on their home than it was worth.

Irene gave Hobie an ultimatum. She was moving to Idaho, where she'd have more success cleaning houses. Hobie could come, or not, but he had to do something. If they wanted to keep their home, they'd have to rent it out to cover the mortgage.

Hobie slinked out of his room and helped move the family to Idaho, where wealthy residents with large estates could use Irene's services, and the Calls rented their house out, hoping to return someday.

Unfortunately, Irene and Hobie found, they were terrible at picking tenants. Their first renters stole the washer and dryer and refrigerator. When Hobie discovered the theft, he demanded that the renters replace the appliances, and eventually, after much cajoling, they did. Then they left.

After spending seven months in Idaho, the Calls moved to West Jordan, Utah, a town just south of Salt Lake City, so they could be closer to the home they were trying to save.

Hobie got a job as an air conditioning repairman and tried to
rent out the home in La Verkin once again.

The new renters paid their first month's rent, which
seemed like a good sign this time. But their second month's
rent never came, and sometime during their third month in
the Calls' home they moved out and left the lights on. When
a neighbor mentioned that he hadn't seen anyone over at the
house in a few weeks, Hobie and Irene went back to see what
was going on. What they found was a nightmare.

The lawn mower was gone. The weed eater. The trampo-
line. The dishwasher. The doorknobs, the light fixtures, the
stove—all gone. And when the renters took the fridge, they
didn't pinch off the water line that led to it, so water had
leaked all over the wood floor, destroying it beyond repair. Finally, as if to add insult to injury, in the two weeks they'd oc-
cupied the home the renters had painted the walls in colors
Irene found quite hideous.

It was time to let the house go. But Hobie couldn't let go
of his athletic dreams.

"The marathon trials were a blessing in disguise," Hobie says.
The winning time was 2:09, and third place was 2:11; it would
have been even sadder to run a perfect race and realize that his
best was still not good enough. Hobie might have retired, but
he got angry instead.

He used that anger to fuel his training for the next year.
A different kind of training that focused more on strength
than logging ninety miles a week and prepared him to go after
world records that were never quite recognized for one techni-
cal reason or another.

Among Call's self-documented achievements: he's lunged

the quickest mile (24:56), logged a 4:40 mile while wearing a forty-pound vest, and run the fastest 5K (17:36) while wearing that same vest. He hoped that someone would sponsor him to dazzle the world with more feats of strength, but when no-body came forth to fund his training, he turned to running again—he could never get the marathon trials out of his head. Perhaps he'd return for revenge.

But in the few years after that Olympic qualifying race, Hobie suffered injuries. A hamstring pull. His knees gave out. He spent 2009 and 2010 trying to get back to that point where he could be a contender for marathon stardom, but just couldn't get there.

"At the end of 2010, I said, 'Well, I'll run a couple of mar-athons in 2011, and if I do good enough and make some money, I'll keep going,'" Hobie says.

But Hobie's body wouldn't go the distance anymore. He'd worn it out. Logging long, cold miles over the winter had blown his knees apart. He finally decided he would retire.

That's when Irene got a Facebook message telling her to check out this strange new event. It was called a Spartan race.

"Hobie said he didn't like to get dirty," Irene says. "It's true!"

Hobie liked running outside, but he didn't want to get filthy—that sounded awful. But after Irene's friend sent her a link to a Spartan event in California, the Calls couldn't stop looking at the website, fascinated by this odd new sport. After digging through the website for a while, they discov-ered something incredible: Joe De Sena, creator of the Spar-tan Race Series, was offering $100,000 to anyone who could sweep the season by winning all fourteen Spartan races.

Hobie could get dirty for $100,000.

He jumped into the family minivan and drove to his dad's home in California, ready to take on Joe's challenge.

Hobie's dad accompanied him to the event, covered by a local TV station. In an interview with the newscaster, the elder Mr. Call told San Diego that his son was going to win the $100,000 award. And when he met Joe face to face at that race, Hobie's dad told Joe the same thing: his son was going to take home the grand prize.

Joe laughed.

Hobie won the Temecula Super Spartan Race by six minutes.

Next up: another Super Spartan Race in Arizona. Hobie drove all the way out to Chandler to win that event too. *Now I have to start trying,* he thought.

The next race was in Texas. Hobie's boss started letting him take Fridays off so he could compete, but traveling to the events was becoming a financial burden. The Calls decided to sell their twenty-two-inch TV to get Hobie to Texas, where he won the race by five minutes, thirty-three seconds.

Hobie was hooked on the sport. "It makes me feel like a kid again," he likes to say. More than a decade after his college running coach censured running off course, it looked like Hobie might make $100,000 doing just that.

To get to the fourth event in Florida, the Calls sold the kids' remote control cars to buy a $400 plane ticket. Hobie won by thirty-five seconds. He was on a roll! He might make his fortune as an athlete after all! So De Sena changed the rules. At least, that's how Irene saw it.

Not only would Hobie have to win all fourteen Spartan races to receive the $100,000, but he also would have to win the Death Race, the grueling endurance event that landed

Daren de Heras in a wheelchair. The event that covers more than forty-five miles, can last anywhere from twenty-four to more than seventy-two hours, provides no race map, and has a 90 percent dropout rate.

But that wasn't all Joe had up his sleeve. Should Hobie win the Death Race, Joe announced, Joe would offer $20,000 to anyone who could beat Hobie in the future. Joe even tasked a member of his staff, Jason Rita, with finding opponents capable of crushing Hobie. It was like Hobie was an obstacle racing outlaw. Wanted: One gifted athlete. A threat to the financial stability of the Spartan empire. Reward for his dethronement: $20,000.

Irene thought Joe was a dirty rotten scoundrel. Hobie figured he never would've attempted a Spartan event in the first place if he'd known he'd have to do the Death Race to win the $100,000. He likes shorter races, two, two and a half hours max. He's built for speed. But he'd gotten this far already. He couldn't turn back now.

Hobie checked off two more races in Georgia and New York. Irene baked cookies and tamales to get Hobie to the first, and De Sena paid Hobie's way to the second, promising Hobie's kids he would buy them a new TV if Hobie lost the Death Race. The publicity this HVAC installer from Utah was generating for the Spartan Race Series was worth the investment in a plane ticket and fifty-five inches of plasma.

Days before the event, a story appeared in the *Wall Street Journal* talking about Hobie and the $100,000 challenge. An enterprising thirteen-year-old boy read the article and decided he wanted to do something to help Hobie. So he presented the story about Hobie's predicament to his father, Rob Eberle, the president and CEO of the New Hampshire–based bank-

ing software company Bottomline Technologies. In the hope
that Hobie would stick it to Joe De Sena, Eberle's company
sponsored Hobie for $9,000.*

Hobie tried his best to prepare his sprinter's body for the
strange and torturous test of endurance that he'd soon face in
Joe's backyard.

There's not much to say about the Death Race, really, Hobie
sighs. It was freezing cold, and when he and other racers tried
to huddle by a fire, it seemed to make Joe angry. The fire's
for volunteers! Not racers! Get away from there! Joe yelled at
them.

Hobie got hypothermic. His body slowed down. He
couldn't stay focused. "I quit at twenty-nine hours," he says
about mentally giving up. "But I dropped out at thirty-seven."
He didn't finish, let alone win, and the $100,000 slipped
through his cold, creaky fingers. A fifty-five-inch flat-screen
now fills his basement.

But all was not yet lost.

Random people sent money after the Death Race. They
loved Hobie. Athletes from CrossFitters to ultrarunners admired him for the way he seamlessly blended strength and endurance. The media loved Hobie and Joe's David and Goliath
story.

Everybody wanted him to keep running.

So Hobie continued to race, having become somewhat

---

* The official reason for sponsorship: "Because just as Hobie goes through mud,
ice, stones and other obstacles to win a race we go to work each day prepared to
go through whatever obstacles are in front of us to delight our customers." Adds
Eberle, "We also thought the idea of trying to stack the deck against him was
not just cowardly but violated the most fundamental basic spirit of any competition—fair play."

Erin, at the start of the Survivor Mud Run

Jimmy Wills

A mud pit at Survivor Mud Run on Dell'Osso Family Farm

Jimmy Wills

Erin with Team Xtreme at the Survivor Mud Run

Jimmy Wills

Will Dean

AP Images/Joe Giddens, PA Wire URN:16436553

Mr. Mouse

AP Photo/Jon Super

Jimmy and Garrett at the start of Tough Mudder SoCal

Courtesy of the author

A runner slithering through Electric Eel at Tough Mudder SoCal

Courtesy of the author

Erin training
in Erik Taylor's
garage gym
Erik W. Taylor

Erik Taylor in
his gym
Courtesy of the author

Spartan Race HQ
Courtesy of the author

Joe De Sena
Courtesy of Spartan Race Inc.

Margaret Schlachter training in
Utah's Diamond Fork Canyon
Forest Call

Hobie and Irene Call
in their backyard in
Erda, Utah
Courtesy of the author

Ray Upshaw at the Ultra Beast

Jimmy Wills

Daren de Heras on the Spartan Race
traverse wall

Courtesy of Spartan Race Inc.

Erin signing in at the Ultra Beast start

Jimmy Wills

David Gonzales of Amphibious Medics

Kenny Stanford Photography

Todd Sedlak at the Ultra Beast start

Courtesy of Spartan Race Inc.

Juliana Sproles and her Tough Mudder entourage

Richard Ricciardi

Erin on the Ultra Beast traverse wall

Jimmy Wills

Erin at the Ultra Beast finish line

Jimmy Wills

of a celebrity in the rapidly expanding world of obstacle racing. People at the events wanted to meet him. To shake his hand. To get an autograph. Hobie wasn't seeking notoriety, of course, but if it meant he might attract sponsors, he could cope with the attention. And one of the Spartan races—a championship event in Texas—promised $10,000 to the first-place finisher.

The gears in Hobie's head started spinning.

So it wasn't $100,000, but it was still a lot of money. The most Hobie had ever made as a marathoner was about $6,000, and if he won that Texas race, he'd make well above that. This could be his chance. This new sport that he'd known about for less than a year could be his final opportunity to fulfill that boyhood dream of becoming a professional athlete.

Hobie quit his job to focus on obstacle racing full-time. He became the world's first professional obstacle racer.

Four months after going pro, Hobie moved his family into their current residence, a modest home his father owns in the rural town of Erda, Utah. Having a lenient landlord relieves some of the pressure to win, but not much. Trips to town in the family minivan are limited to save money on gas,* and there's often little in the refrigerator besides butter and eggs from Irene's eight hens.

Irene makes all of the family's food from scratch, baking eight loaves of wheat bread every week and blending plenty of the wheatgrass drinks Hobie swears by for optimal training,

---

* This rule caused tension when Hobie's six-year-old son, Forest, finally saved up enough money from completing chores to buy a $1 can of Flarp ("this gooey stuff that makes farting noises," Forest says) and had to delay the gratification of Flarp ownership by four days, at which point he was unsure whether Flarp or Pokémon deserved his investment. Spoiler alert: he chose Flarp.

racing, and recovery. She also takes side jobs when she can, cleaning houses and training horses, while Hobie tackles the main requirement of his new profession: training.*

Fellow competitors admire Hobie's efficiency and grace in completing the obstacles even more than his running speed. It's easy to see how he became so skilled if you take a look at his backyard. In the shadow of the Oquirrh Mountains, a string of nine- and ten-thousand-foot peaks that separate Erda from Salt Lake City, Hobie has built a veritable obstacle course.

A freestanding, eight-foot wooden wall sticks up between a chicken coop and a big beige barn, put up to practice Over, Under, Through, a Spartan obstacle in which racers crawl over a wall, under another, and through a third. There's also a rope slung between two trees for rehearsing the Tyrolean traverse, another obstacle, where competitors shimmy across a cord strung over a pit of water.

Inside the barn, Hobie has carved a workout space into piles of old furniture and boxes and boxes of paper. His dad, a math and history teacher, loves genealogy, and all of those boxes are full of his research. Nestled between them is a small wooden model that Hobie made. It's a tiny replica of the home he hopes to build one day.

The gym itself is simple enough. Some rubber flooring, a treadmill. A few weight vests, free weights, exercise balls, boxes to jump on, and a back extension machine. In the corner, there's a trash can full of broomsticks with nails drilled into the ends, for practicing spear throwing, and a bag full of wood blocks with screws sticking out of them. Those are for

---

* Irene's no stranger to an OCR podium either. In fact, she's racing the Ultra Beast.

practicing the log hop, where stumps of varying heights and widths are placed in a line and racers have to hop from one to another without falling. That obstacle in particular has the potential to be an ankle-breaker, so Hobie prepares for it by pushing these bits of wood into the grass and leaping across them, trying not to touch the ground.

Six or so metal swords are strewn about, spoils from Hobie's victories. A few cardboard checks from Spartan Race and Superhero Scramble are tacked to the wall. No doubt Hobie's race-specific training fueled those wins, but there's more to it. In fact, Hobie's training regimen has become somewhat legendary. Case in point: his workout warm-up is forty-five minutes long, incorporating stretching, strength, and calisthenics. It's a workout in itself, a precautionary, somewhat superstitious step Hobie takes to minimize the risk of pulling something. He knows better than anyone that injuries steal podiums more often than competitors.

As for the core of his regimen, Hobie dominates obstacle courses on no more than fifteen miles of running per week and about ten total hours of working out. The running, he says, is mostly made up of high-intensity intervals. The rest of it is a full-body strength routine he invented that's sort of a blend of traditional weight-lifting and CrossFit. Hobie has packed on fifteen pounds of pure muscle since he switched from marathoner to OCR pro—and anyone can follow his unique and proven training method when they buy *Hobie Call's How to Train for Obstacle Racing* workout DVD. Just $20 for two hours of Hobie's special and highly effective workouts, plus nutrition advice!

So far, sales have been slow. But Hobie knows that making it as a full-time pro—more accurately, supporting a family of seven as a full-time pro—requires personality, an entrepreneurial spirit, and an Internet presence. He finds that last part particularly odious, though — Hobie hates computers.

His new career started off with a bang when he won that championship race in Texas, earning a jaw-dropping ten grand. But this year only six Spartan races are handing out checks to the winners, and all but two of those checks — the payouts for the Vermont Beast and the Ultra Beast — top out at $1,500 for first place. Hobie needs to capitalize on his success, like he tried to do with the video. He also needs sponsorship.

He's had some offers. There was one potentially lucrative deal to be the face of a workout recovery drink, but Hobie thought the product was crappy and overpriced. Proper nutrition is very important to him. He turned the offer down.

Just two weeks earlier, Reebok had flown him to Boston to talk about shoes and clothing and obstacle racing. It seems like something might come out of it. Hopefully. He'll wait to see what happens.

In the meantime, he must train. The Vermont Beast and the Ultra Beast are the biggest money races in the series, guaranteeing each winner $5,000. Not only that, but those races count for double points in the Spartan ranking system.* The person with the most points at the end of the Spartan racing season, which culminates in Vermont, gets an additional $4,250.

---

* A complicated system — not unlike the one USA Triathlon uses — of ranking competitors over an entire season. The Spartan points system ranks competitors by their top five finishes in a season (October to September) by awarding points based on their overall placement in their gender at each race. Points are weighted, based on distance and finish time in relation to the winner's finish time. The person with the most points at the end of the season gets the most cash.

Shorter-is-better Hobie needs that Beast victory. As he says, "I'm still one bad race away from calling my boss."

De Sena is lucky to have found Hobie. The scrappy athlete is marketing gold for Spartan Race, the company's own Horatio Alger story.

Even though De Sena crushed Hobie in the Death Race, he wanted Hobie to keep competing in his events. He's been paying for Hobie's travel and accommodations and waiving his entry fees ever since. That way Hobie keeps his winnings without spending them on racing, and Spartan Race attracts more athletes eager to meet Hobie and test themselves against the best.

Tough Mudder didn't have a Hobie. (Though it did try to create a marketable super-fan. See next chapter.) By definition, it couldn't. But World's Toughest Mudder could. The event would draw elite athletes motivated by the ticking clock, and every winner would be identified in the press as a "World's Toughest Mudder champ," giving the athletes and Tough Mudder plenty of exposure. Most important, Will Dean would finally have an event worthy of comparison to Joe De Sena's beloved Death Race. Dean could not pass up that opportunity.

The first WTM kicked off on December 17, 2011, in Englishtown, New Jersey, at Raceway Park, a motor-sports facility that also hosts drag races and motocross events. To enter, athletes had to claim that they'd completed a Tough Mudder in the top 5 percent of all finishers. Since the events are not timed, it was an on-your-honor deal. The process was less rigorous than the essay-based application required for the Death Race and the Ultra Beast, leading some Mudders to complain that they didn't feel special enough for getting in, because anyone could, really.

Nevertheless, 1,004 racers showed up for a chance to nab the $10,000 grand prize. The rules were simple: The man and woman who completed the most laps of the eight-mile, forty-obstacle course in twenty-four hours won. Fail to properly clear an obstacle, Big Mudder warned, and you'd be disqualified ("Big Mudder" being the Orwell-inspired name devotees sometimes call Tough Mudder). Or you'd have to do an obstacle designated as a penalty, like traversing fifteen-foot-long parallel bars suspended eight feet above a water pit using only your hands. Fail that and you'd have to wait in a holding area for five minutes before proceeding. Because it was so cold outside, standing around turned out to be a particularly brutal punishment.

Runners set up tents along the track and shimmied into wetsuits to brave temperatures ranging between 23 and 42 degrees. After a siren sent them off at 10:00 AM, all Dean had to do was wait to see who would become Tough Mudder's new heroes.

One man and one woman set themselves apart early on. On the men's side, Junyong "Pak-Man" Pak was dominating the field. By midnight, the thirty-three-year-old mechanical engineer from Massachusetts was working through his sixth loop, and Juliana Sproles, a forty-two-year-old personal trainer and triathlon coach from California, had gapped her competition by an entire lap.

As the clock ticked closer to twenty-four hours, racers dropped out in droves. By 1:00 AM, only 204 Mudders remained, according to Tough Mudder's live event blog. At 4:00 AM, there were 185. At 7:00 AM, 130. At some point, when there were so few people left, Tough Mudder did away with penalties altogether.

By 10:00 the next morning, only 103 people were still in the race. That would give WTM a finishing rate of exactly 10 percent, equal to what De Sena aims for at his Death Race. That rate, Death Racer Daren de Heras believes, enraged De Sena, prompting him to make his next event harder than ever. De Sena dubbed the Death Race following the debut of World Toughest Mudder "the Year of Betrayal."

De Sena made everything in the Death Race heavier, longer, and more grueling. Where racers previously carried small logs, they now had to carry sixty-pound bags of cement. Short hikes were transformed into epic bushwhacking treks through the forest. Before, obstacles had been merely maniacal. Now they were borderline sadistic.

Take the Roller Coaster, for instance. After the Death Racers had been competing for more than two days straight, race directors ordered them to log-roll six times around a quarter-mile track. Halfway through each lap, racers had to stir a bucket full of rotting cow intestines and other festering bull parts ten times. Some racers puked. A lot. Then they all had to roll through each other's puke.

And as if all that weren't tough enough, the race went on for more than two days straight. Before World's Toughest Mudder, the Death Race had never lasted longer than forty-eight hours. Post-WTM, the final Death Race finishers limped in after competing for sixty-seven hours and fifty-two minutes. De Sena never left the course the entire time; he wanted to ensure that nobody thought his race was too easy.

But WTM had a 10 percent finishing rate only if you go by the official online recap. The official WTM 2011 video, posted on the same webpage, states that 800 people started the race, not 1,004, giving the event a finishing rate of 13 percent. Still pretty tough, but not *exactly* Death Race tough.

Unlike virtually all timed events, however, World's Toughest Mudder did not publicly post racing stats such as average pace, lap, or finishing times. Instead, its website links to a permission-only Google Drive document that presumably shows "final times for the 521 participants who finished at least 1 lap at World's Toughest Mudder." The company refused to grant me permission to see it.

So maybe 521 Mudders did conquer a lap of the freezing course. Maybe they didn't. What's certain is that only one woman completed six laps, or forty-eight miles, and one man finished a seventh lap twenty-three minutes ahead of his nearest competitor. They were the very first World's Toughest Mudder champions, Dean's new stars: Junyong Pak and Juliana Sproles.

Both of them are racing the Ultra Beast.

7

Unleashing the Ultra Beast

RACERS ZIP ABOUT every which way, abuzz with caffein-ated nervous energy. Some are bouncing up and down, trying to stay warm in the cool morning light. Pit crews shake shoul-ders and snatch shucked clothing. Parents chirp kind if mis-guided words of encouragement like "We love you no matter what!" and "Don't die!"

Don't puke! I think, standing at the base of Killington Ski Mountain, staring at the shiny, grassy ski slopes. I haven't been this nervous about a race since I was a freshman on the high school swim team, spewing in the pool gutter before every meet. I couldn't help it, the nerves just bubbled right up out of my stomach. And now I'm right back in the middle of a race day nervenado, trying not to get swept up.

It doesn't help that today's projected high is 70, a temperature this Arizona-bred girl finds pretty chilly. Expect it to be 10 degrees colder on the mountain, Margaret Schlachter posted in a Spartan Facebook group. And windy.

I throw a Hefty bag over my shoulder and march straight toward the transition area, a large patch of grass marked off with white tape.

The trash bag is full of stuff I'll need or might want half-way through the race.* Extra PowerBars and the two glow sticks and headlamp required after 7:00 PM. I threw them in there even though I'm certain I'll be done by then. I also threw in a surgical coat my doctor neighbor gave before I left home when I told him the race might be cold and rainy.

"Here," he said, handing me three coats. "They're blood-proof and windproof, and they keep me warm in the operating room." I told him I'd look like an escaped psychiatric patient running up a ski mountain in an operating gown, but thanks for the thought. I threw one in my bag for backup.

I set the trash bag down by a big turquoise bin with the name MAYNARICH printed across the top, then look around for landmarks that will help me find my bag after the first lap.

There's the spear throw on the other side of the transition area. Bales of hay that look like fat torsos on stick figures. A board mounted at a 45-degree angle with ropes dangling down it. Huge storage containers stacked two high that form the foundation of the rope climb.

The closest thing to my bag is a black wall with bits of

---

* It will also handily serve as my body bag, if need be. It's already tagged with my name on a strip of duct tape.

wood nailed into it, and it's not that close. I decide Maynar-ich's bin is bright enough to catch my attention. Then I figure this entire effort was pointless because the sadists who run this race will probably mix up all of our bags while we're out on the first loop to mess with our minds.

Ten minutes! someone yells over the loudspeakers. I look up at the stage to see a man named Chris Davis standing there. This guy, the announcer roars, lost a crazy amount of weight to get to this race. He started the course in the dark at 4:00 AM, and right now, right here, after nearly four hours of hiking and tackling insane obstacles, he's at mile 4.

"The race directors have shown you all mercy by letting you duck out of the race at this spot—a dignified exit, no questions asked," the announcer yells. "Chris, tell the people how many pounds you've lost!" The emcee is hyping up the crowd with Chris's transformation story, but just when I start to listen—

"Did you sign the wall?" someone asks as I'm herded into a line of people who must write their names and race numbers on a big board, presumably so someone knows we started and will therefore make sure we're accounted for at the end of the day. Someone pelts me with a neon-green sweatband, then instructs me to put it around my arm and to get into the start corral. This race is not going to begin exactly at 8:00 AM.

I peel off a sweatshirt and hand it to Jimmy. His wave doesn't start for another hour and a half, but the elite racers—the ones racing for prize money—start with me. Beast racers, Ultra Beast racers. Hobie and Irene. Junyong Pak and Juliana Sproles. Margaret Schlachter. They're all lined up at the front of the start corral, muscles coiled, ready to spring out ahead.

I check to make sure the rain jacket attached to the back

of my CamelBak is latched on tight. Then I squeeze through a hole in the corral fence and stand in the crowd of more than 1,100 people, all of us with sweaty palms and pounding hearts, revved up to face the unknown.

A group behind me jumps up and down, trying to stay warm, cracking jokes about how this is nuts, how they're going to die. I tune them out, letting my mind slip away. Maybe it's a reflex, like a puke-proofing reaction I've developed since high school, I don't know. I begin to zone out, standing in the middle of everything but not really there.

The announcer says Joe will give free merchandise to anyone who brings Chris Davis a big breakfast of bacon, eggs, and orange juice. A young man with a giant mustache volunteers to play race waiter.

Then along comes a bearded, shirtless guy, squeezing through the competitors. He stands right next to me, towering over everyone around us. I wouldn't have paid him much attention except I know him. He's the guy from Jimmy's Tough Mudder, the one with the Tough Mudder pledge scribbled across his back—the human cue card waves of Tough Mudders turned to for help reciting the credo. Three months later, those words are still there, completely untarnished.

I snap out of my trance. I'd touch his back to try to smear the ink if that weren't weird, but it'd only confirm what I already know: that is a massive tattoo. And the only thing crazier than the tattoo itself is how it got there—and how this human homage to Tough Mudder wound up in the Ultra Beast start corral. (Warning: offensive language ahead.)

To say Ray Upshaw's year was going poorly would be a gross understatement. As the twenty-five-year-old Missourian puts it, "A lot of bad shit went down."

At one point in his young adult life, Ray joined the Navy to make a difference and not "waste four years getting some bullshit degree" he wouldn't use. He served for a year before receiving a medical discharge. During that year, he met a girl who turned into his fiancée. She was pregnant with his child when she was killed in a car crash.

The tragedy put Ray in a funk for a long time. He was angry at the world. "I would just tell people to fuck off because I didn't see anything in people that I liked, and when I did give people a chance I'd get shafted," Ray says. "You can only make an angry snake so angry before he starts fucking people up."

One day while he was browsing the Internet he came across an ad that asked a simple question: Are you tough enough? He clicked through and found the Tough Mudder site. Upshaw liked what he saw: a company all about people helping each other out. "It didn't matter your time 'cause it was so difficult. It had a mentality of 'I don't have to think about whether or not you've got my back as long as I've got yours,'" Ray says, and he loved that. He kept an eye on the company and was impressed when it sold out its first-ever event.

About a month later, Tough Mudder put up a Facebook post that said it'd give anyone who tattooed his entire back with the Tough Mudder pledge and logo free entry for life to Tough Mudder events.* It was a publicity stunt that seemed unlikely to find any takers, but Ray was game. He wanted to be a part of a movement defined by kindness and chivalry,

---

* Tough Mudder still has a tattoo policy: participate in a Tough Mudder, get a Tough Mudder tattoo within one month after your event, get one free entry to a future event. More than 1,000 people have inked themselves with the orange flame logo. Spartan Race's policy is more vague. People with Spartan ink might get something if they were to "email us and put up a good case," says race director Mike Morris.

one about strangers helping strangers and forging new friendships.

It took him about a month, but he finally got in touch with Tough Mudder, which sent him a contract stipulating that he had to get 70 percent of his back tattooed to receive the lifetime event pass. The contract also stated that Tough Mudder would reimburse Ray for the tattoo, while Ray would run Tough Mudder courses shirtless and "assist with all reasonable requests by Tough Mudder for media interviews or photographs at each Tough Mudder event attended."

Before Ray had ever run a Tough Mudder, he sat for six hours under Missouri tattoo artist Jimmy Israel's needle, emerging with a design that looks very much like someone wrote the pledge on his back with a marker, just like obstacle racers scribble their numbers across their foreheads and biceps.

At first, Ray says, Tough Mudder didn't think he was serious enough. Perhaps they didn't believe the art was real, just like I didn't until I stood next to him. So Ray teamed up with a friend who does body suspension to shoot a ten-minute video in which Ray hung from four giant fishhooks that pierced his freshly tattooed back flesh. He sent the video to Tough Mudder with the following note: "I don't know. You guys think I'm serious?" ("What can I say," Ray says, "I like to send a message.") Tough Mudder told him not to send anything like that again. The company sent a $250 check, which covered half of the tattoo's cost; Tough Mudder put a stop payment on the second $250 check before Ray could cash it, he says. The company declined to comment on the matter.

A few months later, Ray flew across the country to do his first Tough Mudder in New Jersey. At that race and for the next few months, everything went the way Ray thought it would. Tough Mudder acknowledged his tattoo, dubbing him its number-one super-fan. Tough Mudder set him up in interviews to promote the company. He spoke with *ESPN The Magazine,* the Weather Channel, and Atlanta's *Dr. Fitness and the Fat Guy* radio show on Tough Mudder's behalf. Tough Mudder even gave him free event entries to share with his friends.

Then Tough Mudder announced it was making a Hall of Fame, a webpage where worthy Mudders would be publicly recognized for their achievements. The only way to gain entry was to run every Tough Mudder held in a calendar year.*

Ray didn't want his tattoo to go down as a gimmick, as nothing more than his fifteen minutes in the spotlight. He wanted to be permanently immortalized in Tough Mudder's Hall of Fame. Tough Mudder wouldn't induct him for the ink, but Ray believed he deserved the accolade and was prepared to do whatever it took to earn a place there. So he went to a second Mudder, and a third Mudder, and the more he ran the more people started to recognize him. They wanted to talk to him. They'd come up to shake his hand and tell him things like "You really helped me get through this" and "You're really inspiring a lot of people." Ray felt loved and appreciated. He felt like he was playing an integral part in building a special community, and that spurred him to continue competing. "I was like, 'All right, I have to finish this out,'" Ray says.

At the time he had been working on a Kawasaki assembly line, and his bosses were "screwing him out of a lot of oppor-

---

* There are currently two more ways to become a Tough Mudder Hall of Famer: (1) Win a Most Respect Award, given to Mudders who the company feels are true heroes. "We admire their bravery, and we think their stories are inspiring," the TM website says. And (2) "Do something that impresses us."

tunities," he says. He was asked to do *Fear Factor,* an NBC
game show that pitted contestants against each other in a variety of stunts for a $50,000 grand prize, but Ray says his bosses
threatened to fire him if he left to do the show. He was also
tapped to participate in a *Maxim* contest, but his bosses said
he'd get fired if he did.

"Well, they didn't really say they'd fire me," Ray says, "but
they said, 'You know what's going to happen if you go,' so . . ."
The final showdown came when his bosses didn't want to let
him leave to compete in the first World's Toughest Mudder. It
was like telling a groupie who went to every concert on tour
that he couldn't go to the final show. Ray went ahead and did
it anyway. Then he ran another Tough Mudder in Tampa Bay,
Florida.

When Ray came back to work, he was suspended for missing more than three days in a week, and then he was let go.
He lost his job on Christmas Eve.

Ray wasn't too worried, however, about his employment
situation. He'd been talking with Tough Mudder about working for them. "Everybody told me, 'Hey, we'll take care of
you,'" Ray says. "Well, being fucking homeless, living out of a
backpack, and trying to make shit work. If that's getting taken
care of, I want to know what the hell isn't being taken care of."

Ray was sleeping under overpasses as he hoofed and hitch-
hiked his way to every Tough Mudder event in the United
States. During that time he emailed the company obstacle designs and asked about job opportunities. "I've probably got
like 6,000 emails from talking to Tough Mudder," he says.

At one point things looked promising. The company set
him up to talk with IDEO, a contractor Tough Mudder had
hired to design some obstacles. Ray shared his ideas but says he
wasn't compensated for the meeting. Then things got worse.

At an event in Beaver Creek, Colorado, local security guards confiscated Ray's backpack after he left it in the Dos Equis sponsor tent overnight. The bag, they said, looked suspicious.

When Ray asked for it back, the guards told him they'd turned it over to Tough Mudder's lost-and-found. Tough Mudder staffers who saw the bag told Ray it had already been shipped back to TM headquarters in New York with the other lost-and-found items. Tough Mudder's chief culture officer, Alex Patterson, ultimately told Ray he couldn't find the bag.

"My entire life was in that backpack," Ray says. "So I said, 'Give me some Tough Mudder apparel, or something.' Then it just turns out they give me fucking nothing," Ray says. With no money and no place to go, he decided to stay with Hobie Call in Utah. "Luckily Hobie gave me a pair of shoes, and my mom mailed me some clothes."

Despite the bag incident, Ray asked Tough Mudder about employment again. "Their main guy told me there's a snowball's chance in hell that I'd ever get to work for them, ultimately because of that video," Ray says. "They don't think I'd fit in with the crew." But that's not the only reason Ray believes their relationship turned sour.

Tough Mudder had recently inked a sponsorship deal with Under Armour worth a rumored $2 million to $3 million. The OCR company and the sports outfitter share a charity partner in the Wounded Warrior Project, a nonprofit organization whose mission is to help wounded service members reintegrate into society.

Tough Mudder declined to comment on its falling-out with ex–Navy man Ray Upshaw, but perhaps TM wanted to focus more on this mutual partner.

Tough Mudder also had elite athletes Junyong Pak and Juliana Sproles to market. Perhaps it wanted to focus on them. Whatever the case, Tough Mudder no longer wanted Ray.*

Joe De Sena heard about Ray and offered to help him out. What could be better than having Tough Mudder's most famous supporter go Spartan? How about filming Ray turn Spartan after helping Hobie Call dominate a Tough Mudder?

De Sena paid a film crew to follow Ray and Hobie as they conquered a Tough Mudder together. The course: Tough Mudder Colorado, where Ray lost his bag. Perhaps Ray's attempt to infiltrate the event for De Sena ultimately led to his shunning.

Fortunately for Tough Mudder, Hobie and Ray did not run fast together. They carried a log and chatted up other runners. Then they stopped to let those runners sign the log with a Sharpie. De Sena never got the footage he wanted of Hobie winning the event, but he still bought Ray a Greyhound bus pass in return for his effort. Worth about $540, the pass would give Ray a few months to go wherever he pleased. De Sena also offered to pay for removal of that enormous Tough Mudder tattoo, but Ray refused.

"The Spartan Races do more for me than Tough Mudder ever has," Ray says. "But I tell everybody, love it or not, I'm married to Tough Mudder. We're together for better or worse." He's still so passionate about Tough Mudder because he loved every one of the events he did and the people he met on course. He's also learned a bit about how the business works from being around it so much, and now he would like a piece of the pie.

"Companies are giving out thousands of dollars to obstacle

---

* Later on, a Tough Mudder representative would tell the *Financial Times* that Ray had become an irritant and a concern for the brand.

racing," Ray says, referring to the Under Armour sponsorship. Ray's waiting for the day when his loyalty to Big Mudder will wind up in a sponsorship deal as well.

In the meantime, he'd like to train people for obstacle races. "What if Tom Brady taught you football? Or Kobe Bryant taught you basketball?" Ray says. "I'm the original Tough Mudder, and I have the drive to be amazing at what I do." He's currently certified under the American Council of Exercise and working on his National Association of Sports Medicine credentials, so becoming an OCR coach isn't an unreasonable goal.

He also wants to be in the top ten in the Spartan points race so he can win some cash to help him start over. Even though he's Tough Mudder to the core, he says he has to do the Spartan Ultra Beast, that he doesn't have a choice in the matter. His reasoning goes like this:

"It's the first Ultra Beast, the first twenty-six-miler. What happens if I don't do it? Sure, most people wouldn't care, but at the same time, what does that do to everything that I've done? I gotta do it. I gotta succeed because, I guess it's a little fucked up to think, but if I can make this work and get all big and famous, this'll be an opportunity to fix my family."

His four sisters and one brother haven't seen him race. "They've all made bullshit excuses," he says. His mom came to one event that was staged close to her home. His dad thinks he's "crazy till Sunday," and that the worst thing to ever happen to him was leaving the Navy. "But maybe I could fix all of that," Ray says, "if I make something of myself with this obstacle racing stuff."

Standing next to me in the Ultra Beast start corral, Ray pulls a water bottle out of his pocket.

"This is all I've got," he says. Well, the water, a packet of peanut M&Ms, and a Beefy 5-Layer Burrito from Taco Bell. The food's stuffed in a Tupperware container in transition for safekeeping. Between me and him, I'm not sure who's less prepared for this race.

One minute!

Jimmy leans over the fence to give me a kiss and whisper something in my ear before he takes off to get photos of the race start. Then people start yelling and jumping around and smoke starts spraying and the crowd starts to move forward, picking up momentum until we're all charging toward the mountain and all I can see is white.

8

In the Army Now

KILLINGTON, VERMONT

SEPTEMBER 22
0815-ish

"MY LEAST FAVORITE part is the smoke." That's what Irene Call once said. It lasts only a few seconds, then the grassy slope appears again. The front-runners sprint straight up the slope while the rest of us march behind. We duck under thick flaps of fabric, then dip right into trenches, giant watery pits separated by mounds of mud. Shoes swell with chilled sludge that rises thigh-high. A shock, for sure, but not bad. The key to staying warm is a dry torso, and though the forecast called for scattered showers, there's not a cloud in sight.

The course clogs with racers as we funnel into freshly cut single-track and wind up, up, up the mountain. We scurry under barbed wire slung between the trees, scale one row of walls, roll under another, then jump through a third. We hike up roads and more single-track, up grassy ski slopes, and in and out of the trees in one big, snaky line of people.

Back in the forest, we face a cargo net hung vertically between two trees. People cling to it like giant spiders while brawny men hang on to the bottom to pull the ropes taut. I scamper over and keep hiking, down and around to two six-foot walls. The boys muscle up, but I grab the top, throw my left leg up, and use it to pull my body over.

I march sideways, right foot first, to take some tension off my Achilles. The technique doesn't seem to slow me down. I haven't done any burpees yet, and I think I'm keeping up since there are people all around me. Then I turn a corner to see a clearing covered in barbed wire.

"Hobie rolls through it," Irene had said. "It's faster." I hang my CamelBak on my chest and start to roll. One rotation in, I hear a man yell, "You don't roll in the Marines! You'll get shot!" I don't know what to do. This is a race, rolling is supposed to be faster, and nobody's shooting at us. We're allowed to roll, right? We're not being recruited for service, right? Wrong. The military is watching, and in my case, it appears, they don't like what they see.

Ray Upshaw was dead-on when he said there's a lot of money to be made in sponsorship — more than he'd have ever made in the Navy. The hard part is creating something worth the cash.

Since around 2002, the armed forces have tied their brands to extreme sports. The National Guard spent $26.5 million to sponsor Dale Earnhardt Jr.'s NASCAR Chevy for a single year. Between 2011 and 2012, it spent a reported $90 million total in motor-sports sponsorships and $20 million on professional fishing. The Navy supports the X Games, whose sponsorships are said to cost between $1 million and $3 million.*

The stated point of all of this sponsorship is to generate recruits, and what better place to find future soldiers than at an obstacle race?

"Usually there's some sort of negotiation where the military will pay X amount of dollars if the event portrays the military and the military participants in a certain way, say, recognizing a particular corps of veterans for the day," says Roger Stahl, an associate professor at the University of Georgia whose research centers on the military and popular culture. "Not just anyone can have a tank."

The tanks parked at Tough Mudders prove the company is working closely with its military sponsors, among whom have been the US Marine Corps, the US Air Force, and the US Army Reserve.

"The demographics of the event do a very good job of mirroring the basic demographics of the Army Reserve, as far as age and education level," says the Army Reserve's recruiting communications chief, Lieutenant Colonel Tad Fichtel. "And of course, both groups are dedicated to being fit."

Over two years, the Army Reserve backed eighteen Tough Mudder events in what Fichtel describes as "a lower-cost sponsorship." In return for bringing in fire trucks, cargo trucks,

---

* In 2012, Congress tried to cut $72.3 million slated for pro sports sponsorships from the next year's $608 billion defense spending budget, claiming the return on investment was negligible. In a particularly damning statement, Major Brian Creech, resource and contracts manager for the National Guard recruiting division, told *USA Today Sports,* "In fiscal year 2012, the National Guard has been contacted by more than 24,800 individuals interested in joining because of the racing sponsorship." Of those, 20 were qualified candidates and none joined. Creech's math was questioned, and the US House of Representatives struck down the amendment, allowing continued sports sponsorship.

and an undisclosed amount of cash, Army Reserve officers got to speak directly to potential recruits. The Air National Guard supports Spartan Race in a similar way.*

This kind of military sponsorship is not limited to OCR; for decades the US armed forces have maintained a comparable relationship with Hollywood. The military will look at a script and let filmmakers use equipment like trucks or an aircraft carrier for free, essentially subsidizing the film in return for Hollywood's help in building their brand. "The military doesn't put its stamp of approval on an event if it doesn't tell the story they want to tell," Stahl says.

That explains why the people behind Steve Martin's *Sgt. Bilko* pointedly did not thank the US Army in the end credits of the film. ("The filmmakers gratefully acknowledge the total lack of cooperation from the United States Army.") A movie about a gambling sergeant who makes fools of his superiors probably didn't win many offers to lend artillery. But an obstacle race that touts its founders' military connections? Of course! Grab a tank or two.

Will Dean often plugs his background as a former counterterrorism agent in Britain, though that experience probably did not involve much physical training. *The New Yorker* described him as one of "the intelligence guys, the ones at the back of the office, analyzing spreadsheets." Tough Mudder's combat cred comes from "consulting input from a for-

---

* Ultimately, the military gets more from OCR than potential recruits. Tough Mudder has donated more than $6.6 million to the Wounded Warrior Project, simultaneously becoming the military charity's largest benefactor and receiving a corporate image boost. And California's Marine Corps Base Camp Pendleton raises more than $1 million annually from its World Famous Mud Run. Held on the base for over twenty years, the event now draws more than 30,000 racers excited to take orders from young men in fatigues.

mer member of the Special Air Service" and a "Tough Mudder employee named Paul Simcox who was a Royal Marine."
The company claims its courses are designed by British Special Forces.

Spartan Race boasted that the Royal Marines created its
courses and that "seven insane ultra-athletes and a Royal Marine" invented the series. But all of that changed in December
2013 when its Royal Marine was outed as a fraud.

In dozens of interviews, Richard Lee, thirty-one in 2013,
had been referred to as "a former Royal Marine Commando,"
but the Spartan UK representative never completed the training to earn the title.

The Walter Mitty Hunters Club HQ exposed Lee's dishonesty. The British organization is run by former servicemen
who investigate people who claim to have served in the military. They say the terminology Lee used while speaking about
his experience in the Royal Marines tipped them off.

"Although he spent a short amount of time in the RM,
he never made it past phase one [of a two-phase program], so
was not able to gain the knowledge in order to convince those
that know," club representative Dave Hart told me. "We trap
most of our Walts this way."

Lee did not appreciate the outing. "Like most Walts, he
tried to call our bluff with threats of legal action, then claimed
it was lies spread by a business rival," Hart said. In the end,
Lee admitted that a broken kneecap forced him to drop out of
Royal Marines training early and that he'd never received the
Commandos' exclusive green beret.

Joe De Sena says he was unaware that Lee hadn't earned
the right to call himself a Royal Marine Commando. He
called the revelation "upsetting" and asked Lee to resign.
Eleven days after the news about Lee's deception broke, Lee

stepped down, leaving Noel Hanna as the only Spartan co-founder with any combat connections. Hanna, Spartan Race says, once served on the antiterrorist squad of the Royal Ulster Constabulary, Northern Ireland's famously dangerous but now-defunct police force.

With such tenuous military connections, these organizations reap huge benefits from military sponsorship. It's a potential source of revenue, sure. But most important, having camouflaged vehicles and real soldiers in fatigues on hand boosts the genuine military training atmosphere many events want to create, because that authenticity draws millions of people to their races.

The next logical question is: Why? Why does saying the Spartan race was "designed by Royal Marines" or that Tough Mudder was "designed by British Special Forces" make people more eager to compete?

Consider these two facts: the United States has been at war since 2001, and the average age of a Tough Mudder participant is twenty-nine. Millions of obstacle racers have spent nearly half of their lives in a country at war. They've grown up in a culture where daily news covers tales of soldiers in training, soldiers on antiterrorist missions, soldiers wounded in combat. The Super Bowl, the most-watched television event in the United States, has featured video messages from soldiers stationed abroad during the halftime show and commercials that depict soldiers in emotional homecomings.

For some people, Stahl says, perhaps obstacle races are like the Susan G. Komen for the Cure events, where people affected by cancer race to empower themselves against a disease that makes them feel powerless. With the United States fighting in Iraq for almost a decade and in Afghanistan for even longer, obstacle racing allows those affected by war to express their pain.

The theory is plausible. One father I met ran six Tough Mudders in sixteen days. His son had just been sent overseas, and this was his way of dealing with the deployment. He wanted to experience the fear and exhaustion that his son was surely feeling at that moment on the other side of the world.

Obstacle racing fanatic Todd Sedlak, aka Sergeant Sedlak, says his decision to retire from the Army in 2006 was a hard one. He had served for more than eight years when he decided he needed to spend more time with his family. He was being deployed constantly and had missed the first two years of his daughter's life.

"It was a really difficult choice, and I struggle with it to this day," Todd says. "I don't know anybody who's gotten out who doesn't miss it, as much as we all bitch when we're in there. There's a camaraderie that exists in the military that is not matched anywhere else. Sports teams are maybe a shadow of that. But putting your trust in someone to make the winning shot is not the same as putting your trust in somebody so you don't get shot." Military people all meet each other on these obstacle courses and swap war stories, so there's that, Todd says. "And it's a simulation of a place in our lives that's missing."

Todd is particularly fond of events with extreme mental challenges. He's completed the Death Race, finishing in sixty-two hours, and he's racing the Ultra Beast. "My wife thinks I'm an idiot," says Todd about his obstacle racing obsession. "But she knows what it does for me emotionally."

People with no direct relation to the US armed forces are still well aware of military culture. It's been a part of most Americans' everyday lives for more than a decade. For them, obstacle racing is less about identifying with soldiers and their pain and more about experiencing what it's like to be one—and people are more likely to play soldier when they don't have to enlist, Stahl says. Especially men. About 75 percent of Tough Mudders and 65 percent of Spartan racers are male. (The American military is even more male-dominated: guys make up 85 percent of active-duty soldiers.) OCR safely satisfies curiosity; it comes complete with all of the camaraderie and extreme athleticism we've seen in the military ads, and none of the bullets or IEDs.

Of course, there are all sorts of nonmilitary reasons why people flock to obstacle courses. A big one: OCR is a rejection of organized sports as we know them. Just like skateboarders in the seventies and snowboarders in the early nineties, says University of Colorado sociologist Jay Coakley, obstacle racers reject the tight regulations and governing bodies of traditional sports.

"There's always a resistance to structure, to something that takes the joy out of it," Coakley says. Sometimes people just need to play; obstacle courses let grown-ups goof off.

Another theory: OCR attracts thrill-seekers and risk-takers—people who crave novelty and variety. Temple University psychologist Dr. Frank Farley calls them "type T personalities." Type Ts love that obstacle courses are constantly changing. It wouldn't be far-fetched to believe that type Ts make up a large percentage of OCR's biggest fanatics.

But it doesn't take a type T diagnosis to become an OCR addict. Researchers believe the human brain is wired to love novelty. New experiences energize and motivate people on an innate, biological level. Conquering new courses and obstacles gives racers a dopamine rush that keeps them coming back for more. Type Ts may simply be people whose brains get a bigger rush from the same experience.

There's also the CrossFit contingent, the more than 10 million strength-based athletes who are primed to compete in groups. Not to mention legions of social media users searching for a way to stand out in a sea of vanilla profile photos and status updates.

It may seem ironic that regimented military types and anti–organized sports rebels love the same events, but that's the magic of OCR: it draws all sorts. The lack of rules, particularly at Tough Mudder, leaves the courses open to interpretation. Participants can make them into whatever suits them. Soldiers can buddy up and impose their own strict standards of conduct, while others can roll willy-nilly under the barbed wire.

No matter how you look at it, though, American military culture has played an enormous role in the development and success of OCR. Which is why it's strange and a little bit funny that without a certain Frenchman, the obstacle course as we know it might not exist.

French people, as it turns out, are crazy about more than American disco music.* They're also nuts about American obstacle racing.

That shouldn't come as a surprise, considering the French created parkour. Both a sport and a philosophy, parkour has been described as the art of getting from one place to another

------

* True fact: The French celebrated their independence day in 2012 by suspending a planet-sized disco ball from the Eiffel Tower's second level, then blasting off fireworks in perfect coordination with "It's Raining Men," "Funkytown," "I Will Survive," "Don't Stop Till You Get Enough," and more for a solid half-hour.

as efficiently as possible. Or, as most Americans would recognize it, the stuff the bad guy is doing while James Bond
chases him in *Casino Royale*'s badass opening sequence: jumping off rooftops, leaping through cars, hurdling fences, scaling
buildings, climbing cables. But before Bond—and before parkour—there was a Frenchman named Georges Hébert who
made it his life's mission to reform physical education.

Hébert was born in Paris in 1875. By the turn of the twen-
tieth century, he had become an officer in the French Navy. As
the story goes, Hébert traveled to remote parts of the world as
a naval officer. To South America. To Cuba.

In Africa he noted the remarkable athleticism of native
tribes. They moved so efficiently, so effortlessly, so nimbly
around any obstacles thrown in their path. And they'd learned
to move so freely simply by being in nature; they'd had no formal physical education. Hébert was entranced.

In 1902, while stationed near the French Caribbean island of Martinique, he witnessed Mount Pelée's eruption,
which swallowed the entire city of Saint-Pierre and more than
30,000 of its inhabitants within minutes. Hébert helped rescue victims of the volcano, and that experience made him realize just how important it was that soldiers be physically fit
and mentally tough to maximize their effectiveness during a
crisis. Not only should they have strength and endurance, he
believed, but they should also use those powers for the greater
social good. And that's how Hébert developed his personal
motto, which has become a central tenet of parkour and continues to resonate with athletes today: *Être fort pour être utile.*
Be strong to be useful. That, he thought, is what the military
should be doing.

Hébert returned home determined to reinvent the way
physical education was taught to the French Navy. His idea

was simple but revolutionary: train the men in a natural environment. Develop their physical fitness with a course—*un*
parcours—in which "one walks, one runs, one jumps, one
progresses quadrupedally, one climbs, one walks in unstable
balance, one raises and one carries, one throws," he wrote.
The course should make people not only physically strong
but also mentally strong. It should teach them courage, will-
power, and resolve. It should teach them morality by height-
ening their emotions. And to that end, it should not be competitive, because competition blocks athletes from developing
sound moral values. Physical development should aid inner
development.

Hébert built an obstacle course for the French Navy—*un*
parcours de combatant—with balance beams, rope swings,
towers of scaffolding, and ladders. He also encouraged people
to train spontaneously in their natural environment.

By 1909, the entire Navy was training under Hébert's *mé-
thode naturelle*—the natural method—and his principles
were spreading beyond the military as he encouraged everyone—both men and women—to enjoy being active.

He'd probably be happy to know that over the years other
militaries adopted his training methods and that his obstacle course remains an integral part of military training philosophies around the world. But he'd probably be even more
pleased to know that the French public—and civilians in
countries all around the world—are now completing obstacle
courses for fun.

France alone has more than a dozen events. There's Le
Crazy Jog, a seven-kilometer obstacle race held at le Stade de
France, the country's national stadium located on the out-
skirts of Paris. The Jungle Run, a series of three urban obstacle courses held in different locations throughout the

year in distances of seven or fourteen kilometers. La Frap-
padingue X'Trem Race Series. The 12K Got Balls? run.
L'Insurmountable. SoMad. L'Infernale. L'Audacieuse. La Dé-
jantée. And now they have Tough Mudder and Spartan Race.
In fact, several non-English-speaking countries currently host
Tough Mudders and Spartan races, including India, Slovakia,
Mexico, South Africa, South Korea, Japan, Hungary, Chile,
Poland, Germany, and Australia.

Perhaps inspired by Georges Hébert's fitness philosophies,
Brigadier General William Hoge introduced the obstacle
course into American military training in 1941 at Virginia's Fort Belvoir. The course, US Army literature states, was
"designed to teach recruits how to handle themselves and
their equipment in simulated field conditions." It incorpo-
rated "walls to climb over, hurdles to jump over, barbed wire
to crawl under, ditches to swing over, and pipes to crawl
through" and proved so effective that similar courses were
soon installed at Army bases around the country. And much
as Hébert originally hoped it would, the obstacle course became a way to teach mental skills, in some cases even more
than physical ability.

     To begin Army training, for example, soldiers must face
a "discriminator"—or confidence builder, depending on how
you look at it. It's an obstacle called the Tough One. To complete it, soldiers must climb a thirteen-foot cargo net, make
their way across logs that are horizontal to the ground and
spaced more than a foot apart, climb a log ladder that nar-
rows as it goes up and tops out at thirty-three feet high, then
scramble down another cargo net to the ground. The course
isn't timed, because it's designed to give soldiers "confidence in
their mental and physical abilities while cultivating courage."

The courses used in the military are usually relatively short, with obstacles often placed back to back. And rather than wearing moisture-wicking, body-hugging fabric or tutus, soldiers tackle the obstacles in full gear: thick boots, abrasion-resistant pants, helmets, and body armor. Just that stuff alone can weigh 35 pounds. Then add water, food, batteries. Some guys can be carrying up to 100 pounds of gear, and once they're all loaded up, they march.

Had Richard Lee actually finished his Royal Marines Commando training, he would have had to complete two marches: a nine-mile speed march with a ninety-minute limit, and a thirty-mile march with an eight-hour limit.*

Twelve miles is standard for the US Army Rangers, who are widely recognized as the nation's most elite soldiers, the guys who are always ready for combat, be it by land, sea, or air. They must complete the march in less than three hours, and when it's done, that's when they tackle "o-courses" like the fabled Darby Queen, located at Georgia's Fort Benning. It features twenty-six of the most difficult obstacles used in military training, crammed into 2,000 meters. The Tough One's in there. So is the Slide for Life, in which soldiers must slide down a rope slung between the top of a forty-foot tower and the top of a ten-foot post to complete the challenge.

And soldiers don't just do the obstacles straight through either. In between, they get smoked—ordered to do flutter

---

* The other two of the four Commando tests are obstacle courses. There's the endurance course, where recruits navigate two miles of tunnels, pools, streams, bogs, and woods, then run four miles back to camp, in combat equipment and carrying a weapon, all in less than seventy-two minutes. When recruits return from the course, they must nail six out of ten shots on target in a shooting test to pass. And there's the Tarzan assault course, an aerial slide, ropes course, assault course, and thirty-foot wall that must be completed in thirteen minutes while carrying equipment and a rifle.

kicks or mountain climbers or burpees—before continuing
on to the next obstacle.

Members of the military have their opinions as to which
o-course is the toughest, but Nasty Nick usually wins the title.
It's located at North Carolina's Camp Mackall and is designed
to just evaluate the soldiers who want to join the US Army
Special Forces by subjecting them to their fears. A climb up a
tall, unstable rope ladder will bring out a fear of heights, while
a crawl through a narrow, wet tunnel will bring out a fear of
cramped spaces. Psychologists watch the soldiers as they navigate Nasty Nick and take note of each one's mental state. Neither of those phobias will fly in the Special Forces.

Military o-courses are completed for a purpose, whether it's
to gauge a soldier's physical readiness to join a more specially
trained regiment or to beef up a soldier's mental game.

Spartan Race embraced the former goal when designing
its obstacles. To get the first events going, Joe De Sena hired
a carpenter in Pittsfield to build the basics: straight walls, in-
clined walls, A-frames for net climbs. During the break between the series' first and second seasons, Spartan employee
Russell Cohen got to work designing more obstacles.

The fifty-four-year-old had been a roving staff member,
filling holes where he was needed. Before Spartan, he'd been
a chiropractor, an adventure tour organizer, and an engineer.
He decided to apply those skills to Spartan obstacle design,
tinkering in his Long Island garage during the winter.

He played around with eye hooks and pulleys, heavy bags,
buckets, and lots of wood. By the time he emerged at the end
of January, he'd invented what would become Spartan classics:
the Herculean Hoist, in which racers yank up a weight tied
to a pulley system; Over, Under, Through; the traverse wall, a

rudimentary bouldering wall; Bucket Brigade, in which athletes fill a bucket to a line with sand, then carry it up and down a hill; the Atlas Carry, blocks of cement that racers must tote a certain distance; and the spear throw. They're all fairly basic but physically demanding challenges.

"The whole theory behind a lot of these obstacles is that the people who do the best in this competition should be the whole package," Russell says. "Not a runner, not a power lifter, but somebody that's got it all."

Now Russell is Spartan's director of building logistics. He shares a Google Doc with the company's employees where they can submit ideas for improving current obstacles and creating new ones, all with the "total athlete" in mind.

Tough Mudder took a different tack, latching on to the o-course's mental aspect. The crazier the obstacle the more buzzworthy and proprietary it becomes. The series' iconic obstacles, including Arctic Enema and Electroshock Therapy, are known for being super-engineered, terrifying, and trademarked.

At least a quarter of all Tough Mudder obstacles carry the protective ® symbol. After all, as Harvard wrote when it sanctioned Will Dean, the public and uncomplicated nature of OCR businesses "makes them largely understandable to bystanders without any special access to proprietary information." The only things setting one event apart from another are brand image and the obstacles themselves.

While early Tough Mudder obstacles seem to have been influenced by Tough Guy creations, Tough Mudder has since invested in its own research and design.

The company partnered briefly with the global design consultancy IDEO and sent Ray Upshaw to brainstorm with the firm. IDEO's crowning concept was for an obstacle called

Break on Through, "in which multiple participants must run full speed into a spring-loaded padded wall simultaneously and knock it over before they can move forward," IDEO wrote on its website. It also came up with five other concepts for "further thinking and design."

That design takes place in a New Jersey warehouse, *The New Yorker* reported. Mark Lombardi, a twenty-eight-year-old mechanical engineer who previously designed nuclear submarines for defense contractor General Dynamics, oversees Tough Mudder's in-house obstacle innovation.

When the *New Yorker* reporter visited, Lombardi and his crew were working on various inventions. In one of them, cannons shot tennis balls into an empty shipping container that Mudders had to run through. It scored high on buzzworthiness in a customer survey, but low on safety: two participants were hit in the eye and one in the neck. The engineers were happy that it became the most-talked-about obstacle on Facebook—a sign, it seems, of a job well done.

That's not to say that Tough Mudder isn't physically demanding, or that Spartan doesn't mess with racers' minds. On the contrary, there's nothing easy about completing a mountainous ten- to twelve-mile course or memorizing Bible verses to repeat hours later in a race. But the different philosophies are evident in the companies' overall obstacle designs.

The trick is to find the sweet spot where obstacles are tough and scary enough that people are challenged but still want to return. About half of first-time Tough Mudders come back again. Spartan Race guards its return rate as a trade secret.

Just like recreational racers, soldiers don't run o-courses daily. They might do one once in the first few weeks of training, then never again.

In the old days, says Army Ranger Ted Holmes,* instructors would pee into o-course mud pits as soldiers sloshed through, but not anymore. "There's no more shenanigans," Ted says. "The point is to make you confident."

One time during training at West Point, Ted had to climb up a wiggly I-beam, then walk across it, trying not to look down at the water forty feet below. It was a big mental test, and he thought it was kind of pointless. But when he got to Iraq, some of the bridges were out, and he had to traverse rivers by walking across trees in his gear. "That stupid I-beam actually paid off," he says. It just goes to show that, "if it doesn't have any training value behind it, we don't do it."

---

* Not his real name. He wasn't authorized to talk to me, so I changed his name.

9

Endurance S&M

HOBIE IS HURTING. Despite his best efforts to avoid injury, he pulled his left hamstring a week before coming to Vermont. He ran too fast downhill, and then the pain set in. Now he's in a battle for first with a mysterious competitor he just can't shake.

Hobie faced Cody Moat once before. At a race in Utah, Cody nipped at Hobie's heels, following his every move until they hit barbed wire three-quarters of the way into the course. Hobie rolled under the spikes like a wheel on a race car, leaving Cody in the mud. Hobie bested his random rival by a solid three minutes, thirty-nine seconds. He hadn't seen Cody since.

Yet here he is again, in the middle of Killington Ski Mountain, completing the obstacles at Hobie's side, totally unfazed by everything thrown their way. Even crazier: Cody's not just racing the Beast, he's racing the Ultra Beast—two loops of this brutal course—and he's still out here ahead of everyone, pushing the pace, breathing down Hobie's neck.

Three miles behind, I'm getting soaked. While I and a dozen other racers are trapped under barbed wire that stretches 300 feet out, a mean man sprays us with freezing water. It numbs my body to the rocks beneath the barbed wire and drenches me to the core.

The next challenge is a hike straight up the mountain. It's tough on the quads, but good for generating heat. We warm up as we march to the top of a ski lift, where a rudimentary set of monkey bars constructed out of metal pipes overlooks miles of pastel-orangey hills.

Those bars might not look like much, but it took a lot of effort to get them up here. The initial planning for an event like this starts six months in advance, when race directors scout for suitable venues. Adequate parking is a must. So is the site's ability to provide the necessary fire and alcohol permits, and the right terrain. Hilly is best, to amp up the difficulty. But the place also must have a clearing for the festival area and flat spots, like the one at the top of this ski lift, where obstacles like these monkey bars or Tough Mudder's Everest can be erected.

In OCR's early years, Spartan race directors would do a Google Maps search to zero in on sites that looked good, then visit contenders to see if they lived up to their satellite images. Now venues like Fairplex in Los Angeles solicit Spartan, while some cities even pay events to come.

A Tough Mudder event held in Whistler, British Columbia, for example, received $112,000 generated through the city's hotel tax and an additional $28,000 from the city's tourism board, according to Whistler's *Pique Newsmagazine*. That made Tough Mudder the third-largest benefactor of the city's hotel taxes that year, behind Ironman ($250,000) and the World Ski and Snowboard Festival ($135,000).

Cities invest in these events because they expect them to bring in people who will shop, dine out, and fill hotel rooms, generating extra tax income. A third-party assessment found that Tough Mudder Whistler drew 25,000 participants and had an economic impact on the city of $4.2 million.

Without subsidies, producing an event can get pricey. Spartan Race and Tough Mudder won't describe the exact cost of putting on their events, but the CEO of a smaller OCR series based in Boca Raton, Florida, will. Superhero Scramble's Sean O'Connor broke down the cost of producing an obstacle event in a post on obstacleracermagazine.com. It went like this:

Site fee: $10,000 to $50,000

Insurance: $5,000 to $25,000

Obstacles: $50,000 to $200,000

Entertainment: $3,000 to $20,000

Freebies (medals/bibs/T-shirts/photos): $15 per racer

Medical services: $5,000 to $20,000

Police and security: $4,000 to $10,000

Advertising: $10,000 to $50,000 [a cost that surely
     shrinks as the brand grows]

Grand total: $132,000 to $420,000 per event

If an event is just starting out, it probably will have to pay expensive site fees. As it gets bigger a city might pay for it. That's the catch-22 of event production: the smaller the race the more it costs out of pocket, but the bigger it gets, the more it can get for free. Kind of like Hollywood celebrities. If Whistler had subsidized the entire cost of putting on its Tough Mudder, and Tough Mudder charged $150 a head, the company would've walked away from the Canadian resort $3.75 million richer.

Once a venue is secured and funding is in place, race directors can plot their courses using Google Maps. But the real fun doesn't start until ten or eleven days out from game day. In Spartan's case, that's when six semis loaded with equipment drop off race supplies: ropes, lumber, pulleys, cement, zip ties, power tools.

Then comes the build crew. Spartan Race has a full-time build crew, while Tough Mudder hires locally. Typically, eight to twelve people start setting up obstacles where the race director wants them, following engineering blueprints and the foreman's instructions.

About five to seven days out, a phalanx of around fifty-five Spartan employees arrives on-site. Throughout the week these staff members, volunteers, and other paid crew members (who are often military) set up tents, generators, light towers, toilets, and water stations. They help the race director mark the course and place T-shirts and medals under the appropriate tents when they're delivered.

Then a day or two before the race, signage goes up. The start sign, finish sign, waiver sign, bathroom banners, medic flags—all of the dressings that make the event look pretty and organized. That's also when the race director does a walkthrough with the heads of the medical and security teams and members of the media.

The day before the race, the race director goes through the

course one more time to make sure everything is just right. Then it's showtime.*

Before the first wave goes off, 800 or so volunteers show up. Many of them are friends and family of racers, or racers themselves, lured by the promise of discounted entry fees. They meet with a coordinator who assigns them to certain tasks. They might man a water station, pass out medals, or help monitor obstacles for injuries. If they're lucky, they become what I like to call Burpee Enforcers, the guardians of honesty who ensure that racers complete all thirty penalty burpees when they fail an obstacle. I meet these volunteers for the first time at the monkey bars.

My wet, sweaty hands can't hold on and I fall. I walk over to the side to pound my burpees out carefully, though nobody seems to be paying attention. Apparently the Burpee Enforcers relax around racers who aren't in contention for money. My Achilles ache, but the pain subsides during the 1,200-foot plunge back to the start line.

The start line. Mile 4. The place to make a "dignified exit" in front of hundreds of cheering onlookers.

So far, so good, I think. Then comes the confidence crusher. Eleven ropes rise twenty-five feet straight into the sky. Men muscle their way up, hand over hand, whacking the bells at the top and scurrying down like it's no big deal.

Now's not the best time to learn that I climb ropes as well as dogs climb trees. Thirty burpees in front of the crowd.

---

* Should the race take place in a stadium, this timeline gets crunched to two or three days. Spartan has hosted events in several Major League Baseball venues, including Boston's Fenway Park, Milwaukee's Miller Park, and Philadelphia's Citizens Bank Park.

Next up: a dip in a freezing pond the resort uses for snow-making. The chances of staying dry at this race, I'm realizing, are low. It's weirdly warm by the shore, but farther out the water is frigid.

Our objective: climb rope ladders that are dangling from a bridge, swing like Tarzan across six short knotted ropes, then hit a bell. Succeed, and we get to swim the short way out. Fail, swim the long way out, and do burpees. I fall off the first rope and dog-paddle the world's slowest fifty feet to land.

Scores of people flop around on the rocks like fish out of water. The damp cold makes our quads and calves cramp while we bust out burpees, screaming with every squat.

Then a lemonade stand appears, just when we could use the sugar most. It's the only aid station providing any calories on this entire loop, but this ain't your typical lemonade stand. Sure, there are cute local school kids manning it. But Joe De Sena wouldn't allow a midrace pick-me-up of smiling children handing out cups of sugary comfort. There has to be a catch.

Five dollars a cup, the kids want. No exceptions. Only people with cash on them or racers who prepaid get the goods. If this is an attempt to divide us—to make the have-nots quietly curse the lemonaders—it's working. If Joe wanted a riot, though, he'd have made the kids sell hot chocolate. The sun is shining, but it gives off no warmth.

Back up, up, up the mountain, the mind games begin. There's a tarp slung between two trees and covered in numbers. *Find the last two digits of your race number,* the instructions read, *then memorize the word and phone number listed next to it.*

Kilo 739-2295. I picture the pattern the number makes on a phone and keep hiking, trying to ignore other racers who are audibly repeating their numbers. *Kilo 739-2295. Kilo 739-2295.*

I'm maybe seven miles in when I witness a desertion. A group of friends who stood behind me in the start corral are trotting back down the mountain, talking about hot tubs and pizza and how this is nuts. They've gone far enough to earn a beer, they declare. They quit!

There's something sad about that moment, but I don't know why. Not until after we scramble over a pair of seven-foot walls and start another 1,100-foot plunge down the mountain and come across Chris Davis. The man who's been out here since four o'clock this morning, racing for his life.

Three years ago, Chris weighed 696 pounds. He had tried losing weight after a thirty-four-year-old coworker suffered a heart attack and passed away. But Chris ended up gaining weight instead, and it looked like he was headed toward a similar fate.

He started having trouble with his legs. They swelled up. Staph infections invaded his body. He was hospitalized three or four times. Imagine getting a rug burn on top of a sun-burn: that's what life was like for him 24/7. Like his skin was getting ready to rip apart.

He spoke with a bariatric surgeon about getting gastric bypass surgery. The doctor told him he had to get down to 600 pounds before he could become a candidate for the procedure, so Chris went on a medically supervised diet. He dropped to 620 pounds and went back to the surgeon, begging him to operate. No luck, the surgeon said. In fact, he couldn't do the surgery even if Chris weighed 600 pounds. The hospital wouldn't allow that type of procedure to be performed on anyone weighing more than 500.

Chris was crushed. He had lost 76 pounds and now he needed to lose 100 more. A friend found a surgeon and a facility that could accommodate people over 500 pounds, but finding the right doctor and hospital was only part of a bigger puzzle. His insurance company wouldn't even consider the procedure until Chris passed a cardiac stress test.

Only one CT scanner in Michigan was certified for people weighing up to 650 pounds. It was new, and Chris became somewhat of a test dummy for it since it had never been used on someone who weighed more than 600 pounds. Hospital executives, doctors, and engineers all came to observe Chris get stuffed into the machine.

Once he was in, Chris had to lower his heart rate below 80 for the scanner to work. His normal resting heart rate at that time was over 100 beats per minute. It took a while for him to Zen out and bring his heart rate down, but he finally did, eliciting cheers from his audience. The stress test was successful.

Chris was cleared for surgery, but his insurance company still denied his proposal. After four rounds of appeals and much emotional torment, Chris finally went into the operating room weighing 634 pounds.

He lost 100 pounds quickly and tried to start working out. It was hard to walk from his house to the end of the yard and back at first, but he stuck with it and eventually went to the end of the road. Then he walked a little farther and a little farther until he pushed it too hard and began to have trouble with his back and knees and hips. So he went to the local athletic center and walked in the lazy river. It took twenty-two laps around the river to go a mile and Chris got up to walking five miles in the water.

He was losing weight and doing well when he got a new computer programming job down south in Atlanta. Determined not to get off track, he joined a running group and showed up to complete a 1.6-mile loop in the local park. The route took him one and a half hours to finish and left him with horrible foot blisters, but he stuck with it, and eventually he signed up for his first 5K walk.

Chris's postsurgical New Year's resolution, he decided, would be to do a 5K event every month. No excuses. And at every 5K he did in Atlanta, he wound up seeing his coworker Shane. Finally, Shane decided that the two of them should try something different, or at least a different kind of 5K. He asked Chris if he wanted to do a Spartan race.

Chris thought a Spartan race was an event held in the town of Sparta about two hours southeast of Atlanta, so he said yes, telling Shane to go ahead and sign him up. Then he went back to his desk to Google the event. What came up in the results was quite horrifying—people jumping over fire! Bloodthirsty gladiators! See, Shane said, that's what you just committed to. Are you gonna do it?

Chris figured there were only two ways this could end. One: he'd get pulled off on a stretcher. Two: he'd cross the finish line and have a great story to tell.

It took him three hours to finish the Spartan sprint. At one point during the race he had to crawl across a cargo net strung over two shipping containers, and when he made it to the top, something inside of him changed. Here he was, a complete computer nerd, climbing up a cargo net. It was something he'd never thought he would do. He was on top of the world! From that point forward he felt as if he could tackle whatever came his way.

By the end of the race he could barely pick up his feet and he was tripping over branches. He was the last person off the course, but it didn't matter to him. He knew his life had changed out there. Completing that event was his reward for losing 308 pounds, and he couldn't have been more proud.

Just one week later, however, his world was literally turned upside down.

Chris was driving to meet a friend at a movie theater when another car hit his Honda Element and launched it up in the air. Chris saw I-85 outside his window, then outside the passenger window, and finally he stopped spinning when his car landed on its wheels and he saw four people running toward him to help him out of the wreckage. Chris was miraculously unscathed, but the accident totaled his car and shook him up. And as if that weren't enough excitement for the month, less than one week after that Chris received a phone call that would change his life. It came from Joe De Sena.

Joe had heard of Chris's accomplishment—that Chris had lost more than 300 pounds before running the Georgia Spartan race—and he was impressed. So Joe asked Chris if he'd like to come to Vermont to train with the Spartan guys for the Ultra Beast. Chris didn't know what to say. He'd been at his job for less than a year, but this was a once-in-a-lifetime offer. Talk to your boss, Joe said, and let me know in two days.

Chris's boss said most people have to quit their jobs for opportunities like this, but he let Chris take a five-month leave of absence to move north to train. So Chris packed up his two-bedroom apartment in seven days, then moved from Atlanta to Pittsfield, Vermont, the tiny town just down the mountain from Killington where Joe and Spartan headquarters are based, population: 546. Living at an inn outside of town for the first three weeks, he was forced to walk five miles to the general store because he didn't have a car. He still doesn't. Now he lives in one of Joe's properties just down the road.

Every week for five months Chris worked out with Joe and the other Spartan Race employees, four and a half hours per

day on average, and the effort paid off. After he moved to
Pittsfield, Chris lost nearly 100 pounds, dropping from 388
to 292. But life in Vermont wasn't all rainbows and butterflies
and weight loss.

Living in Pittsfield was isolating, the thirty-four-year-old
says. In Atlanta he'd go out and explore. He was just starting
to get comfortable in his social life there when Joe plucked
him up and gave him his very own *Biggest Loser* opportunity.
The raw food and veggie diet Joe put him on, Chris says, provides only about 500 to 800 calories per day. He's had trouble
with wound healing. Also depression. He got a skin rash from
the workouts for which he was prescribed steroids, but when
he quit using those, that messed with his brain too. It was all
getting to be too much to handle, and so finally, Chris quit.
He decided he'd had enough. He took a week off to go see his
family—at least that's what he told Joe. But Chris had no intention of going back once he hightailed it out of Pittsfield.

The races brought him back. He likes being at the events,
helping people out. A lot of the time people have trouble at
the sandbag carry, and Chris likes to go out there and talk to
them, helping them get through it and walking with them so
they don't feel so alone. Once they're through that obstacle,
he says, they realize they can keep going.

Joe knew Chris was sick of him, so he started making
Chris march over to Margaret Schlachter's house. She put
Chris through rigorous workouts to help get him ready for his
first half-marathon, a major stepping-stone toward his goal of
completing the Ultra Beast.

He finished that run. It took him nine hours to complete, so he's nervous because the Ultra Beast cutoff is fourteen hours and it's harder and twice as long. But he has to finish this race. He goes back to Atlanta right after this event is

over and doesn't want to leave without following through on that original goal. He promised Joe he'd do it. He promised Margaret. In a way, he also promised his boss, since the Ultra Beast is what brought him to Pittsfield in the first place. Joe even started the race with him this morning, a predawn accountability partner.

After all everyone's done for him to get him to this point, Chris can't go home without a finisher's medal around his neck.

I want to ask Chris if he got his bacon and eggs from the mustachioed race waiter, but figure I'll either sound like a jerk or spoil the surprise. People streaming by him shout words of encouragement, so I do the same and keep trucking. Down, up, and around. In and out of the trees. Alone, but not—there are still people everywhere.

Finally, the trail spits us out at a clearing spattered with ski lifts and a ski lodge. There in the dirt is mile marker 10.

With only three miles to go, this lap should be over in another hour, hour and a half tops. But before we can knock off more mileage, we must face a gauntlet of obstacles. First, carry a sandbag up a ski slope and back down. Next, repeat your phone number—the one posted on the tarp in the trees. Next, pull a sled full of rocks around an oval in the dirt. The sled is heavy, and the dirt is rocky, so the skis don't slide smoothly. And suffocating smoke is blowing into our faces from the fires lit all around the track.

Just as we dump our sleds behind the others, coughing . . . "It hurts my nuts!" someone shouts. It's Ray, making a scene before his second attempt to shimmy across a cable at the Tyrolean traverse, ropes with bells in the middle of them slung across a pit of freezing water, another snowmaking pond. Hit

the bell, drop into the water, swim to the other side, and continue. Don't make it, drop into the water, swim to the other
side, and do thirty burpees. Either way, we're getting wet
again.

Ray and I stand around watching other racers do the obstacle while we wait for free ropes. The pros glide across the
top of the rope, but when a rope to my right opens up, I hang
beneath it, sliding on my knee pit, hand over hand, scooting
my legs, repeat. Once I've developed a gnarly case of knee-pit
rope burn, I reach the bell, punch it, then plunge into the water, leaving Ray and his sore nuts behind.

Three miles left. I trudge through muddy trenches, then
veer right onto a freshly cut trail that leads back into the forest. Twelve hundred feet straight up. No switchbacks, no fire
roads. Just a scramble up the mountain over rocks and roots,
may the strongest quads and Achilles prevail.

This is where Cody Moat makes his move.

Cody Moat has an MO. When he's new to something, he
mimics the pros. Then he outkicks them. The strategy nabbed
him the title of USA Track & Field's fifty-mile trail champion
the first time he ever ran that far, and maybe, just maybe,
it'll make him king of the Spartans. He just has to time it
right.

Hobie's hurting—Cody knows that. The two men have
been chatting, as much as one can when running straight up
and down double-diamond ski slopes. Hobie has mentioned
a few times that his hamstrings are tight, that the guys behind them will push the downhills to catch up. Hobie has
even showed Cody how to get through the barbed wire more
quickly.

"I don't know why I'm doing this," Hobie said, telling

Cody to rotate his fanny pack to the front for a faster roll. Is it a sign? Is Hobie fading?

On every uphill, Cody gets a few minutes ahead, but he can't maintain his lead. Hit an obstacle and Hobie is right there with him, sailing through it twice as fast.

Cody knows his best chance to break away is on a long climb. The father of four from Utah trains by running in the mountains behind his home in Filmore, two hours south of Salt Lake City. He doesn't always take to the trails either; sometimes he just bushwhacks, ten, twenty, thirty miles. It's what he likes to do. He'd run the 5,000 and 10,000 and the steeplechase in college at Southern Utah University, then burned out completely. The mountains, the steeper the better, were his salvation.

He thinks he'll be tough to beat on this monster climb, and Hobie's mental game doesn't seem all there today. When the trail curves into the trees, Cody takes off.

"Oh my God, does this ever end?" A line of us has formed in the forest as we trudge over fallen trees on hands and feet, slow but steady, heading toward nothing. More trail. More up. We hit a traverse that gives us hope. Perhaps there's no more up, there can't be. We zag left for a few minutes, then turn right and *bam!* More mountain.

"I freaking hate Joe De Sena," someone cries. "Yeah!" the crowd agrees. Joe De Sena is one sick guy. No matter that he didn't design this particular course. He's the reason it ex-ists — the reason being out here, climbing like goats up a ski mountain, is an option this Saturday. What kind of nutzo in-vents something like this? Invites strangers to come live with him on the condition that they do this masochistic event? Even weirder, when people say they freaking hate Joe De

Sena, or that he's nutty, they never say it straight. They don't *hate* Joe De Sena. There's always a strange level of admiration and respect backing those words.

Take the pre-race pasta party last night, for instance. Ray Upshaw showed up late because he had to hike all the way there. He'd eaten a ghost pepper earlier in the evening—the whole thing—when no one else would try it, and it had made his throat start to swell shut and the bar he was in didn't have any milk or ice cream, so he had to walk a mile down the road to the market, and then he had to walk another mile to the dimly lit house in the woods where homemade spears lie in the driveway. So that's why he was late. And he was still hungover from the night before.

It was 8:00 PM and three dozen racers were hanging out on the porch. The guest list was a veritable who's who of obstacle racing, minus Hobie Call.

There was Junyong Pak, the small but ripped Korean who'd won World's Toughest Mudder. There was Juliana Sproles, the forty-three-year-old female World's Toughest Mudder champ. There was also a slew of Death Race finishers easily identified by their black Death Race hoodies, including a blonde who didn't look older than twenty-four.

And then there was Death Racer and former Army staff sergeant Todd Sedlak, his right leg encased in plaster, crutches leaning against the porch railing behind him. He'd been sitting on top of the soapy wall—a slick 45-degree wood board that racers climb up with the help of a rope—at the New Jersey Super Spartan Race when he decided to slide down it instead of climbing down the scaffolding on the other side. When his feet hit the ground, his leg shattered into four pieces. The bone was literally sticking out of his skin; he could see it. That was two weeks ago.

The vibrations from people walking on the porch are hurting him, Todd says. Then, in practically the same breath, he says he's going to race tomorrow. "It's the first Ultra Beast, I don't want to miss it." It's like there's an unwritten code that missing this OCR milestone will diminish an elite's legitimacy as a hard-core competitor. No excuses.

The racers are talking about everything from McDonald's mustard packets for sodium to the pressure Juliana feels to do well tomorrow to why the heck they're racing. "We do it for those who can't," someone says, while Morgan McKay, that young blonde with a braid across her forehead, says she races the most grueling events "to prove that you can accomplish anything you set your mind to." She even rolled through puke with her friend Anthony Matesi to make her point. They did the same Death Race as Team SISU's Daren de Heras.

Joe De Sena himself was out on the course imploring racers to give up, trying to get Anthony and Morgan to betray each other by leaving one another behind. You'll never finish officially, Joe told them. Best give up now, there's no point in going any further. Joe probably said the same things to Hobie at the Death Race, trying to break him, to plant a seed of paranoia in his mind that he'd fail.

To anyone in the outside world, Joe's actions would make him a jerk with a capital J, a forty-two-year-old schoolyard bully, a madman even. But not to obstacle racers. They talk about coming to Pittsfield—the town down the mountain where Joe and Spartan headquarters live—like pilgrims talk about visiting Mecca. It's an honor to be invited to stay in Pittsfield, to train with Joe. It's an honor to have him try to break you. A bit of endurance S&M.

10

Injury Report
Not Just a Flesh Wound

THE BEAST/ULTRA BEAST
MILE 10
1020-ish

LESS THAN THREE MILES left. Maybe even less than two.

At this point Hobie deserves to curse Joe De Sena more than anyone. Joe's the reason Cody Moat, an unassuming high school drafting and carpentry teacher, showed up to race in Vermont and is now poised to take down the king. Because even though Hobie didn't win that $100,000 prize, Joe never took his man Jason Rita off the job of finding Hobie a rival. Rita put his money on Cody.

Cody gaps Hobie on that 1,200-foot ascent, but not by much. Hobie's not going down without a fight. When Cody emerges from the woods, he makes a beeline for a rope climb set up at the top of a ski lift, but Hobie never lets him out of his sight. Up and down the rope Cody goes, taking off just as Hobie arrives.

Should Cody be pushing it this hard right now? He still has another lap to run. Coming into this race, he didn't know if he could win the Beast, but he was confident he'd win the Ultra Beast. Maybe he should just save it. But he's *ahead,* and he's great at running downhill. They have to descend this mountain at some point.

Cody dashes along a flat dirt road to the log hop, the obstacle the Calls practice in their backyard with pieces of wood pushed into the grass. Cody cautiously leaps from log to log. Doing burpees now could mean the difference between first and second—a difference worth $3,000.

Hobie mounts the logs behind him just as Cody nears the last one. Then the favored champion says something that makes Cody's confidence soar.

"Since you passed me on this one, I don't think I'm gonna win this."

Sincere? Maybe, maybe not. There's still another 560 feet to ascend and obstacles to conquer before the 1,500-foot dive down to the finish line. And just before the end, the two men will face an obstacle called the Hobie Hop. Hobie invented that obstacle; nobody should be able to beat him on it.

Less than three miles left. Maybe even less than two.

The chiseled guys around me climb the ropes with their arms like it's nothing, but I drop. Thirty burpees. I'm just finishing off the last few (*twenty-eight . . . twenty-nine . . .*) when—

"Erin!"

It's Jimmy, coming out of the trees. Seeing him immediately breaks my race trance, a fish-eye focus on the thing just ahead of me. I should be happy he's there, all smiling and cheery, but he started an hour and a half behind me. *An hour and a half!* I look down at my watch and start running numbers. That goat trail took an hour to climb. I've been out here for four and a half hours already. *Four and a half hours to go eleven miles!* That fourteen-hour cutoff is starting to look less generous with every step. Jimmy worms up the rope, then walks with me.

"Man! That climb was killer!" he says.

"Yeah," I say.

"I'm so happy I found you! I can do the rest with you!"

"Okay," I say as we walk toward the log hop.

"This is awesome! I'm pretty sure I'm first in my wave!"

"Then why are you walking right now?"

"I just, well, I don't care. I'd rather do it with you."

"Go! You can't let them beat you!"

"Are you sure? I have been going back and forth with this one guy—"

"Yes! Go!"

Jimmy gives me a peck on the cheek, then takes off running.

He's gone when I get to the log hop, rows of skinny logs, all about thigh height. Objective: leap from log to log without falling, or twisting an ankle.

It sounds easy enough, but the irony of OCR is that the most innocuous obstacles cause the most carnage. Case in point: a Tough Mudder mud pit sparked a norovirus outbreak in Michigan.* Health officials believe that an infected person contaminated the muck, passing on the illness to everyone

---

* Symptoms were stomach pain, nausea, diarrhea, and vomiting.

who raced after him. A month later a run through the woods near Chicago left about 1,300 Spartans scratching poison ivy rashes.

Those runners were lucky. Other racers have suffered worse on equally straightforward parts of the course: lacerations, broken bones, concussions, heart attacks. A twenty-one-year-old from Michigan named James Sa dove into a Warrior Dash mud pit and emerged a C6 quadriplegic, paralyzed from the chest down. Others have lost their lives.

In the first four years of OCR's existence, five people died. That's a low number considering that more than 3 million people ran an obstacle race during that time. That makes the odds of dying at an obstacle race somewhere between the odds of getting struck by lightning and winning the lottery. Triathlon, in comparison, lost forty-six out of 3 million participants over a nine-year period.

The rarity of OCR deaths, however, doesn't make them any less tragic. Two racers suffered heat stroke at a Kansas City Warrior Dash, one suffered a possible heart attack at Extreme Rampage in Lexington, Kentucky, and two drowned — one at the Original Mud Run in Fort Worth, Texas, and the other at Tough Mudder West Virginia. The Tough Mudder's name was Avishek Sengupta.

The twenty-eight-year-old posted his final Facebook status on a Saturday at 7:39 AM. It said, simply: "Mudder time . . ."

Sengupta and five of his friends were preparing to drive from the Baltimore area to Gerrardstown, West Virginia, to run their first Tough Mudder when Sengupta keyed the update into his phone.

The men arrived at the venue later than they'd expected, but it was still cold outside when they climbed into the start corral around noon — 52 degrees, with bone-chilling twenty-three-mile-per-hour winds.

"It started off fine. It went as well as you could expect," says Josh Muskin, one of four teammates who had met Sengupta while working at a small digital marketing firm called WebMechanix. The fifth teammate was one of Sengupta's childhood friends. The men, ages twenty-three to thirty-four, completed the first obstacle, a barbed-wire crawl, then scrambled over wet, muddy mounds in an obstacle called Mud Mile before climbing up hay bales.

About two miles into the twelve-and-a-half-mile course, Sengupta and his buddies came upon obstacle number four: a twelve-foot plunge into a freezing pit of muddy water. It's called Walk the Plank.

"They sent you off in waves," Muskin says. "You'd get to the top of the platform and stand there, and they would count down for that line of people to jump. Then they would wait for those people that jumped to get out of the way of the next people, and then they would send off the next group."

The obstacle is designed to test the runners' fear of heights. "Don't think too much before you leap," Tough Mudder's website says. "You'll hold up everyone else, and the volunteers at the top of the platform don't like to babysit Mudders."

Muskin says he was the second person from his team to plunge into the murky twelve-foot-deep pit; Sengupta went fifth. He leapt into the water and never resurfaced.

His friends shouted frantically to rescue staff that Sengupta hadn't come up. "At that point, seconds feel like minutes, and minutes are hours," Muskin says. It was just too hard to tell how long Sengupta was underwater.

When the diver finally found him, he was unresponsive. EMTs started CPR right away and continued until an ambulance came to take him to the local hospital. "When I saw him, as soon as I saw him, you absolutely knew there was no hope," one of Sengupta's friends told a West Virginia newspaper.

Walk the Plank was closed for the rest of the day as the local sheriff's department investigated the incident. Doctors at Virginia's Inova Fairfax Hospital took Sengupta off life support the day after the run, saying that the lack of oxygen from being submerged for too long had swollen his brain. He was gone.

Sengupta's death made national news. Until then, Tough Mudder had presented an irresistible paradox: it was the safest most dangerous event in the world, just like Tough Guy. Yes, people ran through 10,000 VOLTS OF ELECTRICITY! but miraculously, they never died. The obstacles *seemed* scary, but they wouldn't actually end you. Everybody kicks back a Dos Equis at the post-event party.

Unfortunately, that's not true. While Sengupta's death uncovered safety issues at water obstacles, ER doctors from Allentown, Pennsylvania, revealed more concerns about Tough Mudder's electric obstacles.

After thirty-eight Mudders flooded their emergency room in one weekend, the doctors put together a report on the injuries they treated.* It became the first published case study on broken Mudders, and it wasn't pretty.

The ER docs focused on five patients in particular, four of whom suffered injuries on electric-shock obstacles. Electroshock Therapy zapped an eighteen-year-old Mudder thirteen times, leaving his back and right arm covered in burn marks.

---

* Marna Rayl Greenberg et al., "Unique Obstacle Race Injuries at an Extreme Sports Event: A Case Series," *Annals of Emergency Medicine* 63, no. 3 (2013): 361–66.

Doctors believed he may also have suffered a heart attack and discharged him with a final diagnosis of myocarditis, or an inflamed heart, caused by electrical shock.

A twenty-eight-year-old was sent home with pericarditis, or inflammation of the fluid sac surrounding the heart. The culprit: electrical current injury. Both types of irritation can disrupt the heart's normal rhythm.

Tough Mudder's electric obstacles can cause more severe injuries than Tasers, the doctors concluded, particularly if runners are shocked when they're already exhausted.

Obstacle courses clearly create endless ways to get hurt. So how does OCR survive in the world's most litigious nation? A country where people sue for getting scared at haunted houses?*

Two words: death waivers. That's what Tough Mudder calls the liability forms each entrant must sign before setting foot on the course. These four pages of legalese include an assumption of inherent risks and a promise not to sue for ordinary negligence resulting in personal injury. All races have similar contracts with lettering in caps or bold when it comes to accidents: COVENANT NOT TO SUE . . . WITH RESPECT TO ANY AND ALL INJURY, DISABILITY, OR DEATH.

It's hard to argue that a racer wasn't aware of the inherent risks when he or she signed and initialed a four-page document while standing under a giant banner reading DEATH WAIVER. Or when, at some point on the Tough Mudder

---

* In 1998 Cleanthi Peters went to the Halloween Horror Nights haunted house at Universal Studios with her grandson. Two years later, claiming the experience had caused her "extreme fear, mental anguish, and emotional distress," she sued the company for $15,000. The case was settled out of court.

course, the racer ran by a sign that said REMEMBER YOU SIGNED A DEATH WAIVER. It's funny if you're still alive, but it also helps secure Tough Mudder's innocence in court should something go wrong. So does social media.

When Spartan Race and Tough Mudder started in 2010, Facebook was blowing up. By July—two months after Tough Mudder and Spartan Race debuted—Facebook had 500 million active users. By the end of 2013 the social networking site had more than doubled, hosting more than 1.2 billion users.

At the same time technology was making it easier than ever to share photos and video. Smartphone sales skyrocketed in 2010,* putting cameras in the hands of hundreds of millions of people who were now ready to document anything at a moment's notice. And GoPro's HD Hero hit the market in 2009. The "world's most versatile camera" made it easy to film spectacular first-person-point-of-view shots in just about any extreme environment. Even on an obstacle course.

All of this technology made experiences a hot commodity. Not just experiences, but proof of experiences. Recount a crazy weekend at the water cooler and you net an audience of maybe twenty, half of whom think you're full of it. Post a photo or video of yourself leaping through four-foot flames, emerging from a trough of neon ice water, or collapsing under the shock of an electric wire while five of your best friends run by in horror and become an online celebrity.

The world of extreme sports in particular developed a "proof or it didn't happen" ethos once GoPro lowered the cost of capturing insane stunts to only $200. As Robert Moritz at *Popular Mechanics* put it, the GoPro "created a virtuous circle

---

* Technology researcher Gartner Inc. says that global smartphone sales shot up 72 percent in 2010, to 1.6 billion phones sold.

of video reinforcement that defines and motivates the culture of extreme sports."

More than anything, people want to show off what they're doing and who they're doing it with. Social media now lets them broadcast their exploits on a greater scale than ever before possible.

Obstacle racing was made for this share-happy, show-offy new world, and event organizers have taken advantage of it. Spartan Race employs professional photographers to shoot its events, then stamps the photos with Spartan logos, throws on a gritty filter, and gives the images away for free. Racers proudly display them as profile pics and cover photos, effectively becoming brand ambassadors.

Companies no longer have to rely on traditional media for promotion. Racers follow their favorite events on Facebook and Twitter, where event organizers shape their unique cultures through a constant stream of branded images. Like a photo of a man wearing a Tough Mudder headband over a curly orange wig and a bra with two stuffed dogs in it. Caption: "Nice puppies #toughmudder."

Events can talk straight to their fans, and fans set up groups where they can stay in touch with people they meet at races all over the world, offering each other encouragement and advice and sharing war stories complete with photo and video evidence of their accomplishments.

But that free flow of branded media serves another purpose, if inadvertently: it makes it next to impossible for participants to claim they didn't know what they were getting into. Race websites are splattered with footage of people swimming across freezing ponds, carrying logs, and slithering through tight tunnels.

Tough Mudder doesn't advertise Electroshock Therapy's

10,000 volts of electricity just for shock value. Everyone con-
templating running through that trestle of dangling wires
knows that's what they're up against. If it gives them heart attacks, it's not Tough Mudder's fault.*

Likewise, when a runaway tractor tire nearly beaned a
Spartan racer in North Carolina, the company dubbed the
thing "Ted the Tire" and posted a video of the incident on
YouTube, #fearnotire. Hard-core? Check. Funny? Yes. Helpful in the event of a tire-related lawsuit? Maybe. The video has
more than 250,000 views.

"A judge will look at it and say the type of accident that
happened, the type of event that caused the injury, was something foreseeable and within the contemplation of anybody
who signed up for the event," says personal injury lawyer
Daniel O'Brien. "If that's the feel the judge has, then he'll
typically rule the waiver will bar a lawsuit."

That doesn't mean races are completely off the hook. Gross
negligence is still on the table. Lawyers Gerald and Kathleen
Hill define the term as "carelessness in reckless disregard for
the safety or lives of others, which is so great it appears to be
a conscious violation of other people's rights to safety." More
than simple inadvertence, gross negligence is "just shy of in-
tentionally evil,"† and it is the core issue in every OCR injury
lawsuit.

James Sa, the young man who was paralyzed after diving
into a Warrior Dash mud pit, sued the company for more
than $15 million. His lawyers cited gross negligence, claim-

---

* Unless the voltage that day was higher for some reason. Injury related to the
advertised 10,000 volts probably won't warrant a lawsuit, but a 20,000-volt injury could.
† An apt description of many Tough Mudder obstacles and probably the entire
Death Race, though not necessarily from a legal standpoint.

ing the race emcee encouraged participants to dive into shallow mud.

Red Frog, Warrior Dash's parent company, responded by quoting a few lines from the liability waiver Sa signed before participating: "I assume all risks associated with competing in Warrior Dash" and "I agree not to dive into or enter the mud pit head first."

Red Frog then asked for summary judgment, a legal move that would've kept the case from going to trial. The judge refused, saying it was plausible—"though barely"—that Warrior Dash's actions did amount to "willful and wanton misconduct." After more than ten months of back-and-forth argument, the case was still ongoing.

Avishek Sengupta's mother filed a wrongful death claim against Tough Mudder nearly a year to the day after her son passed away. Ironically, the technology that helped build up OCR companies like Tough Mudder could also bring them down: Mudders on course with Sengupta caught the tragedy on video, giving unfiltered insight into what happened that day.

A crowd of about fifty people stood atop the Walk the Plank platform, thirteen or so across, four deep. Sengupta leapt off in a wave of seven people. As soon as his friends exited the water, they realized Sengupta had not come out and started yelling at the lifeguards to search for him.

Two minutes passed before lifeguards ordered the rescue diver into the water. Another two minutes passed before the diver got on his fins and mask to begin the search. All the while, Sengupta's friends were screaming at them. A man can go only about four minutes without oxygen before brain damage sets in. One of Sengupta's friends jumped back in to speed up the rescue effort before the lifeguards forced him out.

It took the diver another four minutes after entering the water to find Sengupta. At that point, Sengupta had been submerged for about eight minutes.

In their wrongful death suit, *Outside* magazine writer Elliott Woods reports, Sengupta's family argues that "Tough Mudder failed to implement adequate crowd control and lifeguarding protocols, making an effective rescue impossible and contributing to Avishek's death."

Tough Mudder denies any wrongdoing. The company says it had more than seventy-five safety personnel on staff the day Sengupta died. "This is the first fatality in the three-year history of the company, after over 50 events with more than 750,000 participants," read a press release. "At Tough Mudder, safety is our top priority . . . we have fully trained medical staff on-site."

Those statements may not help Tough Mudder avoid a lawsuit, but they are true. Part of Tough Mudder's magic is, after all, that everyone parties together after experiencing the rush of facing death and *surviving*. In fact, when the company was just starting out, it was so concerned about safety that it commissioned EMT Mike Donoghue to reinvent how on-course emergency services operate for OCR.

At the time Donoghue was a corporate pilot, running a small company on the side called Amphibious Medics. The Los Angeles–based operation staffed construction sites and reality TV sets, including Bravo's *Top Chef*, with first responders. It wasn't a bad business, making about $250,000 annually in revenue and employing four full-time staff members. Then along came obstacle racing, and it changed everything.

Donoghue had to create a system that would bring together seventy-five strangers in the middle of the wilderness to form a self-contained 911 response system. Every weekend. He went from working with a few hundred independent contractors to more than 10,000, all across the country.

Nobody else was equipped to do that. Before OCR, such a system wasn't needed. It was logistically insane, but Donoghue cracked the code and cornered the niche market. In three years, his business ballooned to a $3 million operation. Donoghue quit his pilot job to focus on Amphibious Medics full-time, staffing most of the Tough Mudder and Spartan Races around the United States.

"Nowhere in the history of the world did any company take tens of thousands of people, at one time, in the middle of nowhere," Donoghue says, "and hurt a good percentage of them."

SUPER SPARTAN RACE
WINTERGREEN SKI RESORT, VIRGINIA
0540

Fifteen EMTs gather in the medical tent, a large white structure erected in front of a wooden shack labeled THE WEINER HUT. David Gonzales set the tent up yesterday while guys on the build crew—the group that assembles the obstacles and carves out the course—tried to guess his age. They pegged six-foot-three David at forty-five. He's twenty-six. He has tattoos on each wrist of a weak pulse that gets stronger as it nears his hands, and he's in charge of the Amphibious Medics personnel at Spartan events. He's the guy runners will never meet if they're lucky but are lucky to meet if their race goes awry. David's ready to roll with two walkie-talkies and backup batteries tucked into a leg holster, Lara Croft style. He's his own walking command center.

It's pitch-black out, save for a purplish-brown haze in the distance. The med tent overlooks Virginia's Blue Ridge Mountains, not a bad place to hang out for a weekend. Six of the medics who will be David's "rovers" jump into three rugged terrain vehicles to drive around and get a feel for the course.

0645

David briefs his medics on today's race. It's eight miles long with twenty-six obstacles. There will be 4,500 participants, released in waves of 200 max every fifteen minutes—*woman down!* David hasn't even finished his brief when the first casualty is called in. A lady running the Hurricane Heat hurt her knee. David dispatches one of his medics to pick her up.

Back to the briefing. The race starts with the elite heat at 8:00 AM; then the rest of the runners will be released in waves of 200 max every fifteen minutes until 2:00 PM.

0700

A man wearing a shirt that says OPERATION ENDURING WAR-RIOR approaches David. Similar to the Wounded Warrior Project, the nonprofit seeks to honor and empower wounded service members. Today, fifteen wounded veterans will be racing this course with two dozen OEW supporters. "We have a triple amputee, double amputees, single amputees," Scott Blough tells David. They'll have a Special Forces medic with them, but Scott wants David to know they are out there anyway. It'll be impossible to miss them. Bagpipe players will send them off, and the fifteen wounded vets will be wearing gas masks. "It keeps us all anonymous—we don't want recognition," Scott says. "It's a symbol of suffering."

0715

The calm before the storm. Typically, there aren't a lot of injuries in the elite waves, so the EMTs have a while to take in the scenery. Athletes start to wander around, showing off interesting apparel choices. "Some things you wish you could unsee," says Chet, an EMT from Long Island, New York, as a racer wearing a Speedo and a koala bear hat walks by. At an adult-themed event in Florida, another EMT chimes in, the runners were naked.

0849

Hell breaks loose. The racers disturbed a beehive in the woods at mile 2, and the angry insects are stinging everyone. Volunteers stationed at each of the obstacles radio David when they need help, then David dispatches his roaming EMTs for onsite triage and transportation back to the medical tent.

David sends a rover to check out the situation, but the RTV headed to the hive stalls out on a steep uphill, stranding two of his medics with the bees.

David jumps into his rig, a monster four-door Kubota, to rescue the women while sending the Wintergreen Resort Ski Patrol to the scene. They spray the hive with brake cleaner and pray that'll tame the bees for now.

0915

Priority call on the first obstacle, a chest-high wall. In walkie-talkie code, bad injuries are called "priority," while minor wounds are "nonpriority." With radios all over the course, racers and spectators can hear what's going on. That's why walkie-talkie code also mandates that users stay calm. "Priority call to obstacle one" sounds a lot better than "Holy crap, this guy's ankle is f***ed up! Get someone over to obstacle one now!" Because that's exactly what has happened. This dude's ankle is definitely broken. After the young twentysomething is dropped off at the med tent, he tries to get up and walk around. He wants to find his girlfriend, who was watching the race.

He'll be ambulance ride number two. Another guy never made it to the medical tent; an ambulance transported him straight from the sandbag carry to the nearest hospital, forty-five minutes away.

1000

Five ankles have been through the med tent already. A South African man sits in a fold-up chair with an ice bag wrapped around his swollen left foot. It's at least twice its original size. That first obstacle did him in too. This is his first obstacle race ever.

That ain't nothin', Wintergreen Ski Patrol says. When Tough Mudder held an event here two years ago, they treated a guy who busted out his front teeth falling on a balance pipe.

After half an hour of icing in the med tent, the South African hops away on one leg.

1053

A rover drops off a man at the medical tent. He slipped on a bridge in the forest about three miles in, landing straight on a nail. It appears to be lodged in his right knee. When he bends his leg, blood gushes out, prompting a little girl who sees it to turn to her mom and say, "Mama, I don't ever want to do this race!"

The medics bandage him up and tell him he'll need a tetanus shot.

"Do I still get my T-shirt?" he asks. "I'm running again tomorrow."

1135

Priority call at the eight-foot walls. ALS* (ambulance) requested. David and the ski patrol roll out. David and his team are only allowed to do triage: clean out cuts, ice swollen parts, hand out salt water and ibuprofen. Local ALS services handle the big stuff, like administering IV fluids, asthma meds, and insulin. They work together to make sure all the Mudders get the care they need.

The eight-foot walls are far down the mountain, almost seven miles into the course. EMTs arrive to find a twenty-four-year-old man lying face-down in the tall grass next to the first of two walls. Volunteers say that he has been dry-heaving, and that he said his back and legs are cramping. He said he hit his head earlier in the race and kept going.

David asks the racer if he knows his name. The man nails that one. What about where he is? He's at an obstacle course. Two for two. What about the date? Vague question. Sometime in August? the man says. He's not wrong. Then he starts crying. The ALS team puts him on a backboard and drives him off of the course on a specially rigged quad. David is heading

---

* Stands for Advanced Life Support.

back to the med tent when he gets two more ALS requests: one for an EpiPen, another at the water obstacle.

1157

A man is already strapped into a gurney by the Water Hurdles, a shallow pit with tubes strewn across, when David arrives. Any obstacle with water above the head requires special water-rescue EMTs, but this course doesn't have deep water. When this man stumbled out of the Water Hurdles, he was having trouble breathing. Then he started gurgling and slipping in and out of consciousness. He had a weak pulse. His wife had been running the race with him, but they got separated. The ambulance heads to the University of Virginia hospital in Charlottesville, down the mountain and forty miles away.

None of the medics at this race were present when Avishek Sengupta died, but the death haunts them just the same. Like many of the racers, they operate as a team. When part of the team suffers a loss, it weighs heavily on all of them. Ask these guys about the incident, and tears well up in their eyes.*

1348

The seven medics manning the med tent tend to a record number of busted racers. "This course is hard!" says one who

---

* Amphibious Medics will eventually be named as a defendant in the wrongful death suit against Tough Mudder, along with the rescue diver on-site that day, the facility where the event was held, and General Mills, whose Wheaties brand sponsored the Walk the Plank obstacle. Just before the 2014 season started, Tough Mudder fired Amphibious Medics and hired NYC Marathon and NYC Triathlon medical director Stuart Weiss to oversee its medical operations.

gashed his right knee on barbed wire. "It sucks!" He's smiling. He wants to go back out, but once a racer gets hauled to the med tent, there's no backsies. EMTs cut off his timing chip, standard procedure. He looks more hurt now than when he came in with that bloody knee.

The medics' operation is efficient and friendly. Many of them know each other; they've worked obstacle courses together before, all of them recruited through Craigslist and Facebook and word of mouth. At $75 a day, the gig promises extra cash, but they usually just break even. Gas and lodging aren't included, and some of these guys drove more than seven hours to be here. They do it anyway, leaving family for the weekend, because they like being a part of the event just as much as the racers do. None of them have done a race yet, but they've all overcome their own obstacles. One young mom is in remission from leukemia. Another has a rare joint disorder.

"I love it here because people are happy," says one EMT. "Beats working a disaster."

1752

The Water Hurdles gurgler's wife stops by. The hospital is releasing him, she says. Everyone's relieved. When the race organizers hear that he's okay, they'll be thankful too. That includes Norm Koch, this course's designer. He stayed up past midnight a few nights ago, bushwhacking the course. Later, at an all-staff dinner, each Spartan employee will have the chance to give a shout-out to someone who helped him or her over the weekend. Koch will tear up as he thanks two team members who wouldn't let him bushwhack alone in bear country.

Their efforts were worth it: Koch's favorite thing ever is

when racers say to him, "You suck!" because his course is so
gnarly. But nobody likes it when participants go to the hospital. Everyone lets out a sigh of relief at the good news.

1830

Operation Enduring Warrior approaches the end of the
course. Bagpipes blare as they climb over a soapy wall, then
regroup to face the flames and Spartan warriors together.
Todd Love is out there, now a veteran Spartan racer. The
twenty-three-year-old Marine corporal was on patrol in Afghanistan in 2010 when an IED vaporized his legs and mangled his left arm. He did the rope climb all on his own. Now
he rides on the back of one of his comrades, ready to add another Spartan medal to his collection. There's not a dry eye at
the finish line.

2051

The course cutoff is 9:00 PM. Almost all of the medics are staying in a hotel forty-five minutes away, but still, they don't leave.
They want everyone to be able to complete the course. Flood-
lights come on, illuminating the finish area and the med tent.
It looks the same as it did when everyone arrived this morning.

2200

The last racers cross the finish line. The medics and all of the
Spartan employees cheer them through. They've seen 185 patients today and overseen five hospital transports. Usually
they see only about 100 people at a race of this length. The

event is already going down as one of the toughest in Spartan history, with more than 4,000 feet of climbing in just over eight miles. Tomorrow is going to be even gnarlier.

DAY 2
0715

Roll call. Today there will be 1,400 racers. The first point of discussion is about radio etiquette. "Never say it's quiet. Never ever," David says. Whenever anyone says it's quiet, someone inevitably screams *Medic!* Today the resort will be running a six-man chairlift from 9:00 AM to 3:00 PM. It's nice for spectators, but more important for the medics; it'll help them get racers out from a treacherous section of the woods where a big chunk of yesterday's injuries occurred.

0845

All quie—it's qui—um . . . nobody's hurt yet.

0957

One of Spartan's hype men gets the party started with a sermon on the mount. "You are gonna cry on that hill! You're gonna cry on that hill! You'll say, 'I'm gonna die!' You're not gonna die. I'm telling you, you gotta reach down. For twenty-two years, I've learned to read people from a distance. Your posture tells people what you're made of. Embrace each other! Tell the course, 'You will not defeat me!' I'm sending two hundred fifty soldiers into battle—two hundred fifty well-trained machines. Say to yourself, 'I do not quit! I don't stop!' Anybody seen the movie *300*? Embrace each other!"

Bad analogy? "The thing about the movie *300*," says one medic, "they all died."

But their sacrifice made the Spartan army bigger and stronger.

1045

Priority call near the sandbag carry, two and a half miles in. David sends out a rover and Wintergreen Ski Patrol. When David arrives on scene, a beefy man who looks maybe twenty-eight is sitting in the bed of an RTV, fighting back tears. "This is my first compound fracture," he says. He calls his wife on a cell phone. "I slipped," he says. "Then I heard my ankle pop." It's definitely broken. David runs to find the man's checked bag so he'll have his ID at the hospital.

1234

A twelve-year-old boy has scraped his finger. He's beaming as he walks up to the med tent. "Can I frame this?" he asks his mom, pointing toward his number. "It's my first one," he says to all of the medics. They are appropriately impressed.

1248

A young woman walks in. She has a problem, but it's kind of embarrassing. She turns around, puts a knee up on a chair, then lifts her shorts up over her butt. "A bee stung me. Can you see it?"

1421

Priority call, finish line. A woman got all the way to the last obstacle—the Spartans—without getting hurt. Then right at the end, she put a hand up to protect her face from the pugil stick and *bam!* broken wrist. The medics splint it with cardboard. She's a nurse, she'll drive herself to the hospital.

1700

David picks up a fourteen-year-old boy who was racing with his father. They are the last people on the course. David knows because the Spartan sweeper, Andi Hardy, is running with them, a neon-green-clad, bleach-blonde cheer squad of one.

The boy strained his ankle in the woods. He starts high school tomorrow. He's upset that he's not going to finish, but he has to think about his basketball season. "I'm definitely doing another race," he says. "I want to finish with my dad."

1957

Despite seven-plus-hour drives back home, the EMTs stay until the last racers finish. All of the Spartan staff members join them as the *Rocky* theme song blasts over the loudspeakers and the final three Spartans get their medals. Just like the announcer said early in the day, they had looked that course right in the face and said, "You will not defeat me!"

They are thrilled to have conquered the course. They're proud they never gave up. They remind me of the legions of racers who wandered into the medical tent this weekend with medals around their necks.

"I'm not crying because I broke my thumb," one man said, tears of pain and pride trickling down his dirt-caked face as he presented a swollen hand to the medics. "I finished, that's why I'm crying. I finished with a broken thumb."

SPARTAN ULTRA BEAST

MILE 12

A volunteer points at the ski slope, a black diamond run called Superstar. There's no real trail, just an open, steep clearing covered in rocks and slick grass. I'm 3,746 feet high, looking out at a sea of muted fall colors, and the only way to go from here is down.

The footing is unstable, forcing me and the guys around me to crab walk sometimes. When we get to a road, the white Spartan ribbons direct us back into the woods, where we hop through trees and over wet roots and rocks, down, down, down, with no end in sight. I'm starting to get tired, just a little. I want to be done with this loop, this one loop. It's taking forever. I watch my footing and keep descending, quad breaking all the way.

Finally, we pop out of the trees to find the Hobie Hop. A man gives us thick black rubber bands to put around our ankles, then instructs us to hop over a series of horizontal logs and under ropes. Task complete, the Hobie Hop guard lets us move on.

The mountain isn't as steep anymore. Now we're on a worn trail that zigzags through the woods. An announcer's voice bounces through the trees, though it's hard to make out what he's saying. Dozens of us wind down the trail until we see a familiar scene: the start line, the transition area, the rope climb.

I grab a spear and chuck it at a straw torso, but not with enough thrust to stick it in. Thirty burpees.

Jimmy is cheering for me. People are everywhere, cheering, doing burpees with me, chucking spears. I'm right in the middle of it all, still on track.

Two big men latch on to my wrists and yank me over the soapy wall, the slick 90-degree slope that snapped Todd Sedlak's ankle.

"Thank you so much!" I say. Then they run forward, and I make a move to follow them when a volunteer asks, "Ultra Beast?"

"Yes," I say. He motions to my right, where the course loops back to the transition area.

Everyone is streaming forward. All of those people I had been hiking with, doing burpees with, tackling obstacles with, none of them are turning right. Not one single soul.

They were all doing just one loop, like Jimmy. Where's everyone I started with? I don't see anyone in transition. Am I the last person out here? Where did Ray go? Matt B. Davis? Daren?

If this were a triathlon, I'd be able to gauge how far behind I am by looking at how many bikes are on the racks. Now I can look only at the faces of the people watching me bend over my garbage bag to rip it open. I see pity. No shouts of "You're the first [or second, or third] girl!" to let me know I'm still in the game. Just close-lipped, eyebrow-raised smiles of sympathy.

I glance at my watch. It took me exactly five hours and forty-five minutes to complete that first loop. The course cut-off is fourteen hours.

"You're doing great!" Jimmy says as he comes up along-side my transition bag. It's still there, resting against Maynar-ich's bin. Maynarich probably rummaged through his stuff hours ago.

I tear into the garbage bag and look at my things. I grab three PowerBars, jam one into my mouth, crack two glow sticks, stuff my headlamp into my CamelBak, and march on. I don't have any time to hang out. If I want to make the cut-off, I have to keep moving, because if there's one thing I've learned over the years about going long, it's this: don't stop. You don't have to be fast. You just can't stop.

"Go, Erin!" Jimmy shouts as I head back out toward the trenches. But when I'm not even out of his sight, Death Race finisher Morgan runs by with someone else. *Runs.* Out of no-where. I recognize her light blond hair. I don't know how she got behind me, but she's determined not to stay there. I couldn't have done this without you, she's telling the guy jog-ging next to her. She wants to finish strong. Then they dash off into the forest, and I'm alone again. Totally, completely alone.

And that's when I hear it. A sound, almost like a hissing. Like someone's trying to say something. A single word. Echo-ing throughout the tunnels. One word. One name. Repeated over and over again.

11

This Is the End

JUST KIDDING! THAT'S a line straight out of *The Hunger Games.** That's what it feels like out here. Like I'm Katniss in her first Games, trying to keep it together. Except I'm all alone. No hot boys are fighting for my affection, I don't have a stylist, and I've just proven to be a pathetic shot. To top it all off, my head's not in the game. My brain goes to an ugly place, reeling, filling up with traitorous thoughts.

I don't want to do all of that again. Not another lap. I want to jump into a hot tub with Jimmy. My legs ache and I'm hungry and I'm sick of being wet, and this is quite possibly the worst idea I've ever had. I'm not in the thick of things, I'm at the end. The last person out here. Last and alone. So completely alone.

What's the point? What's the point of racing if I'm not . . .

---

* *Mockingjay,* end of chapter 21. The word repeated over and over again: *Katniss.*

racing? My mom would tell me, *You need to fix that bad at-titude,* but not now. She'd rather I weren't out here anyway, beating myself up, taxing my endocrine system.

What exactly am I doing? Screw the story! I've gone far enough for that. Jimmy won't care if I don't finish. Maybe he'll be disappointed, but not in me. Maybe he'll be sad be-cause we were here and I could've kept going and we might never be back. Just like Race Across Oregon . . . I don't want another Race Across Oregon. It's a long way to come, to the other side of the country, to quit.

I need a mantra. Something to repeat to wash away nega-tive thoughts.

Just chill. I used that one at my first Ironman after a friend told me to "just chill" during the swim so I wouldn't freak out when 2,000 other people tried to crawl over me. It worked. I glided through the chaos in Tempe Town Lake, my smil-ing face making it onto the official race video. But the word *chill* is sending shivers through my body. *Just stay warm* won't work; there's no ring to it.

We do this for those who can't. That's what one of the elite racers said. We do these things, these crazy tests of endurance, for people who can't. For people who would give anything to be hiking in Vermont right now, using, taxing, feeling every part of their bodies. Soldiers race for fallen comrades. Broth-ers and sisters race for family members fighting AIDS, MS, cancer. For friends with broken bones and kidney stones and disabilities. Disadvantages. Our strong, disease-free bodies are a blessing. *A gift from God,* Ryan Hall would say. One that we should never take for granted. We must use them. We must push them to their full potential.

I think of my dad, of how much more difficult this would

be for him. If I bonk,* I feel like crap. If he bonks, he dies. It's not fair. It's so not fair.

When I was younger, I'd convince myself that if I kept going faster, kept going harder, just kept going, there would be a cure for diabetes. That an evil Arctic sorcerer had the answer and had trapped it in a spell and if I could just cross that finish line without holding anything back, my effort would unlock it. The fate of every defective pancreas was in my hands—I just had to finish.

But that doesn't work anymore. My dad could do this if he wanted. It'd be a pain in the butt dragging testing equipment around and trying to clean off muddy fingers for pricking, but it could be done. Anyway, he probably wouldn't want to do this race. And he certainly doesn't want me to hurt my healthy body trying. To destroy the good tendons I do have. Those Achilles would heal if I'd just let them.

We do this for those who can't. Scott Jurek's mother had MS. The famous ultramarathoner watched her slowly lose control of her own body. I wonder if that made him want to run faster, to run farther. To exert more control over his body to make up for her loss.

We do this for those who can't. It's just not working. Those who can't, at least the ones I know, wouldn't want me out here annihilating myself in their name.

Maybe I should just turn back. The more I think about doing another loop the dumber it seems.

I haven't settled on a race mantra or a reason to keep going when I arrive at the spiderweb in the trees. The giant cargo

---

* AKA "hit the wall," aka deplete the glycogen stored in muscles and the liver that's used to fuel activity.

net hung vertically in the forest. There's one volunteer guarding it, and she looks uneasy about sending me up and over by myself.

I didn't think much of this obstacle the first time, so I start to climb. When I get to the top, I'm suddenly aware of how high I am, and how wobbly the rope is without anyone hanging on to the bottom to tighten it up. I swing my leg over as the volunteer audibly inhales, then pick my way down the other side. "Good job!" she says as she high-fives me. Then I weave back into the trees, alone with my thoughts, still fighting that internal deserter.

I'm the greatest! I'm a machine! That one simply won't do either. Today I'm clearly not the greatest. I'm a torn-up lump of flesh. *I'm the greatest! I'm a machine!* Camp counselor Rick used to say that as he chugged along trails in Northern California, leading me and about a dozen other thirteen-year-olds on backpacking trips in the mountains. Perhaps I'll make a quiet, "dignified" exit when I get back to the rope climb. I must be headed that way now, since I'm going downhill.

Then a vision of Erik's gym pops into my head. *The Erin Project.* All of that time he put into preparing me for this race, telling all of his clients what I was going to do. He told me to visualize myself conquering this race. I told him I was when all I ever saw was black. A dark, damp forest. Wet leaves falling. Shadows in the night. No finish line. I never saw a finish line.

I think about Hobie's gym. The kitchen where he makes his wheatgrass drinks. Hobie's stories of how hard he's worked to be here, of how much his family has invested in these races.

I think of the hilltop just north of here that Joe and George and I stood on at sunrise only a month ago. Jimmy cringing as the podiatrist zapped my feet with a sound-wave jackhammer. Chris trying to sneak away from Pittsfield. Chris on

this mountain, racing today. Robyn's kidney stones set in plat-
inum.

It's strange, really, when you sign up for a big endurance
event like this. Or a marathon, or Ironman, or Ultraman. You
start out with an ostensibly selfish goal: I want to do this. It's
going to cost a lot of money and take a lot of time to get
there. Some people sign up to help charities through their adventures, to raise awareness and money. To physically fight
against something that makes them feel powerless. To miti-
gate the selfishness. To have a reason to run that's greater than
themselves so they don't wind up alone in the forest questioning their purpose in the middle of a race.

But a funny thing happens along the way. The race really
does become something bigger than you. It isn't yours anymore. It belongs to everyone who helped you on your jour-
ney. Everyone who inspired you. Everyone inspired by you.
Everyone who believed in your goal too, who saw something
special in it, or in you, even if you didn't.

I can't let them down. I'm physically capable of finishing
this; Erik gave me the quad strength. I just don't want to keep
going because I hate being cold and everything hurts and I'm
alone and I'm sick of being alone in the woods. *I like to do
things I don't like to do.* Joe De Sena sucks.

*You're stronger than you think you are. You can do more than
you think you can.*

Where did that come from? Did the announcer say that
before sending us off into the smoke? Did Jimmy whisper
that to me before I jumped into the start corral? *You're stronger
than you think you are. You're stronger than you think you are.*

I come around on mile 4 again, only this time it's more
like mile 17. I duck under barbed wire, then mount the traverse wall. Hit the bell, then jump into the water under the

ropes. Tug on the rope, then dive straight into a set of burpees. If I couldn't climb that rope the first time, my biceps won't do it now.

People are cheering and the announcer is yelling, but I don't think any of it is for me. Other racers must be streaming over the finish line. Beasters. Ultra Beasters. I don't know. I do my last burpee, then head back out.

"Erin!" Jimmy shouts.

"I'm fudging finishing this!" I shout back. Only, like Ralphie Parker from *A Christmas Story*, I didn't say *fudge*.

I crawl under two kids' obstacles, and then I see it. A row of people doing burpees on a hillside. *People!* Oh my God! I want to hug every one of them.

"Thirty burpees," a volunteer says to me. "The lake is closed."

"It's not our fault the lake is closed!" my mud-crusted compatriots and I grumble to each other as we pound out burpees. "I would have gone swimming!"

That is absolutely not true. Burpees are much warmer than that lake, and it's getting late in the day. The sun was never very cozy at its zenith, and now it's falling down the sky.

The notes of a string quartet playing Jason Mraz's "Lucky I'm in Love" waft through the trees. I can almost make out the wedding that put an end to the Tarzan rope swing obstacle. The bride apparently didn't want people trudging in and around the pond. Guests are sitting on the other side by the Killington Grand. What marvelously photobombed wedding photos that couple will have, with the silhouettes of muddy troll people streaming through the woods behind them.

"You're doing the Ultra Beast alone," a man next to me says. I can't tell if he's telling me or asking me.

"Yes!" I say. "My husband did the Beast."

"He didn't do the whole thing with you?" the man says. "What a pussy."

"Ha!" I say, then I let him go ahead of me. I can't keep up with him anyway.

"Hobie didn't win?" someone else asks another racer.

"I think somebody beat him," the other person says.

"No way!"

No way! I hope they're wrong. Who could've beat Hobie?

A team of three men dressed in black stop so one of them can distribute NoDoz and fuel to his buddies. Caffeine sounds like a good idea.

I pull a PowerGel out of my CamelBak. The edible slime is disgusting because it's so salty, but I probably need the sodium, so down the hatch it goes with a water chaser. I must lament out loud about my terrible decision to leave my ibuprofen in transition, because another man tells me that he and his team will stop in a bit, and if they have any extra, I can have some. It's like an on-course drug deal.

"Thank you!" I whisper.

"It's so nice to be around people!" another man behind me says. I almost jump, caught red-handed. Like he might be an undercover narcotics officer trolling for NSAID offenders. "For a while there I thought I was the only person out here."

"Me too!" I say.

"Peter," he says.

"Erin." We don't shake hands; they're bloating and dirty.

"So you're doing the Ultra Beast?"

"How did you know?" Do I look that bad?

"The green sweatband."

I didn't know that's what distinguishes Ultra Beast racers from Beasters. Now I start to look at everyone's arms.

"You too?" I say.

"For a while there I thought I'd quit, but it's helping to have people to talk to." You and me both, buddy. You and me both.

"Where are you from?" I ask.

"Outside of Boston."

"What do you do when you're not rolling in mud?"

"I own a cookie company."

"No way!"

"Yes way."

"Did you bring your cookies to munch on?"

"No."

"What? Why not? What's your company called?"

"Wicked Good Cookies. I figured if you're going to have a cookie company in Massachusetts . . ."

"That's a good name!"

Peter and I chat all the way to the memorization board. I don't even have to look at it. *Kilo 739-2295.* Couldn't forget it if I wanted to. I charge down the path toward the Herculean Hoist, buoyed by the chat with Peter and the twenty-five-milligram shot of caffeine.

I grab the rope at the Herculean Hoist to pull a concrete block off the ground and set it down again, then turn straight into World's Toughest Mudder champion Juliana Sproles. I can't believe it. What the heck is she doing back here?

Juliana is happy to see another woman on course. So far I have seen exactly none. Or one, counting Morgan's flyby at the beginning of this lap.

Juliana and I and her entourage of three beefy men start hiking at about the same pace. Something, I know, is clearly off if she's back here with me.

Today just isn't her day, Juliana says. She was alone for a while and bummed out until she met up with these three

Tough Mudder guys who look like they could screw my head off my body like a lid off a jar. Sounds like we all started this lap with mental crises.

We walk together, all five of us. We pick up concrete blocks—sixty pounds for the ladies, ninety-five for the men—waddle across the grass with them, then put them down.

When we get to the barbed wire, Juliana and the guys take turns holding strings of spikes up to make it easier for each other to crawl under. The men launch Juliana and me over the first seven-foot wall. Juliana gives me a boost on the second, then somehow manages to scramble over on her own. The boys will make it, she says. We continue on together, talking. It's strange and wonderful at the same time to be making friends in the middle of a race. There's no podium or money calling; we're way too far behind for that. We talk about her kids and her hometown as we climb log retaining walls and hike up and down the ski mountain.

Just before that gauntlet of obstacles where Ray was yelling about his nuts, I hang back to pee on the side of the road in the waning sunlight. A very long pee.

It's entirely possible that someone will come around the corner to see more of me than they ever wanted. But nobody comes, so I stay there, squatting, staring at a flattened mustard packet lying in the road.

We run the gauntlet in the last fingers of light. Sandbag carry, sled drag, Tyrolean traverse. Burpees, check, and more burpees. Juliana slips behind. We assume she'll catch back up and keep marching. Right turn into the forest to begin that epic ascent. Right turn into darkness. The sun has set, and it's black in the trees. I click on my headlamp and pray that it stays on. I never checked the batteries after grabbing it out of a closet at home.

"Stay with us," Juliana's Mudders say. "Let's do this to-gether." It's nice that they've adopted me as their protégée. It makes me feel all warm and fuzzy that these complete strang-ers care about my safety in this forest. I try to stick with them, but my legs just won't go that fast and I fall back. They stop for food, and I catch up. But when they start again, I can't keep pace.

"I'm okay," I tell them. "Keep going."

They slowly pull away until all I can see are their glow sticks, dangling against a shadowy black backdrop.

You're stronger than you think you are. I do an internal check. I am not cold. I'm a little hungry. My legs are throb-bing. My arms are throbbing. All of that pain masks any aches in my Achilles. I can't even tell if they're hurting; my mind's too overloaded with soreness signals from everywhere else. I can see the green twinkle of glow sticks up above and be-low me, letting me know I'm not alone. I'm not the only bear food out here.

When I get to the boulders and jog left, I find more peo-ple. Lots more people. They spot my armband in the light of their headlamps.

"How much farther to the top?" they ask. They must've started in the last Beast wave.

"I don't think we have much more," I say, and I'm right. Soon, we emerge from the trees, headed toward the rope climb at the top of the ski lift.

"Go, Erin!" I hear. It's Jimmy again. Same place as last time. He hiked all the way back up the mountain to cheer for me.

I glance at the ropes, then start to do thirty burpees, slowly, for the eleventh time today.

"You're doing awesome!" Jimmy says as he tries to take photos of me doing burpees in the dark, documenting my insanity for friends and family. "How are you feeling?"

"I'm all right," I say. "I'm gonna finish this."

I have to pee again. I drop trou in the weeds on the side of the road, watching headlamps in the distance, praying they won't turn and shine my way before I'm finished—I don't want to flash the only full moon other racers will see on this cloudy night.

When tendrils of light reach toward me, I reassemble and continue on to the log hop. The balance obstacle. I stand on the first log and contemplate stepping to the second. I'm only maybe two feet off the ground, but I feel like I have vertigo. I can barely stand there without falling off. I don't want to twist an ankle. I'm hurting, but I don't think I'm hurt, and I don't want to get hurt this late in the game if I can help it. I step down and start to do burpees in the grass. Thirty burpees, for the twelfth time today. At least they're keeping me warm.

"Do you know how much more we go up?" a woman asks.

"I think it's just beyond where we can see, but don't hold me to it," I reply. The woman starts to walk with me.

"I hope it's not much farther," she says. "We've been having a rough time." She's competing with an enormous group of women from all over the country who met through social media, she says. And one of the women has been trying to quit, like, forever. Like at every obstacle, she's been trying to bow out, but they promised they'd all finish together, so that's what they're trying to do. This woman next to me really, really wants to finish. She hopes there's not too much left so her teammate won't have any more excuses to give up. Keeping her going is wearing the team down.

"You guys are really close," I tell her. It's kind of a lie. They're close to the top, but not to the finish, but who's counting? I want to believe me too.

"You're doing the Ultra Beast?" she says. "That's amazing. Good for you."

"Thanks," I say as we approach what I thought was the top. But there's more mountain. That must make this lady angry, because I think she just spit on me. Or snot on me.

"Oh my goodness, is that rain?" she says.

It *is* rain. Just a sprinkle.

"Good luck!" I tell her, picking up the pace. *I can't get wet.* I keep going up and up. *It's just sprinkling, you'll be okay.* I climb over a boulder covered in cargo net and keep marching, and just when the eight-foot walls at the top of the mountain come into sight— *deluge!* It's pouring! Freezing cold rain. We're all getting soaked.

My body immediately freaks out. I panic. I have to get off of this mountain *now.* I get hypothermia in cold rain.* *Just keep moving, you'll be fine.* I look around. There's no one behind me to help me up the walls. No more strong men or Juliana to give me a boost. I don't have the strength to go it alone. My biceps cramp just looking at the obstacle.

I walk up to the volunteer, who's panicking himself. Like he's going to turn into a frozen humansicle if he has to stay out here in the rain too. He wants to get off this mountain pronto.

"Where should I do my burpees?" I ask.

---

* LA Marathon, 2011. It was 55 degrees and pouring rain. EMTs pulled me off the course at mile 24. After an hour of lying naked under a plastic blanket pumped full of hot air while a handsome doctor periodically checked in on me, I left the hospital like nothing had happened.

"You know what?" he says. "This is a burpee-free zone. Get out of here."

I turn and look down Superstar. The Killington Grand lights glimmer in the distance like Christmas lights in the snow. That's my hotel. The one with the hot tub and the sauna and a warm bed. The only thing between me and it is this ski mountain. An entire freaking ski mountain.

I sit to inch my way down the slope. I don't want to fall. A man comes up next to me and launches himself around me when he loses his footing. He starts to tumble and doesn't stop, bouncing down, down, down the mountain on his butt like Superstar is a waterslide. A runaway Spartan! I watch in horror, picking my way toward him, when, finally, a rock stops his fall.

"I'm bleeding, but I don't know where from," he says.

I don't know what to do. It's like a war of the gods out here. Like Zeus dumped a giant bucket of water on this mountain to try to wash us all off of it. I scoot by the bleeding man on my hands and feet. There's nothing I can do for him. I keep going, slipping down this grassy slope of death, drenched and cold.

Then the course veers into the trees. What once was a trail is now a waterfall. There's a blurry glow from a steady stream of green glow sticks in the black rainy forest. It's all I can see, besides the few feet in front of me. It's quiet here, except for my breath. The breath of my fellow racers, gleaming sticks in the night. The muted sound of the rain falling through the trees. Our feet in the thick, deep mud. The water trickling down the mountain.

My body is calm here in the forest. I can't feel it anymore. I don't feel pain. I don't feel cold. I don't feel hungry. I'm a part of the stream. A part of these trees. A part of a warm energy emanating from the people around me, whose presence I feel, but who I can't really see as we slop down, down, down. Over roots and rocks and running water.

When a few of us slip out of the trees at the Hobie Hop, I know we're going to finish. There's no way we can't finish now. We jump the logs, then return our rubber bands to the volunteer.

I take off running when we get to the last trail through the woods. As fast as I can, my legs start to spin, feet splashing in the water. I feel like I've never been injured. Time slows down as I speed up. I hear my breath. The sound of wet leaves falling on the damp ground. Of splattering water. I can't see the finish, can't picture it even, but I know it's there and I keep moving forward. *Just keep moving.*

A man runs behind me, quietly floating through the night in my footsteps, and in this moment I know that Jimmy was right, all those weeks ago, when he said that I would suck at this. That I have to race because racing is a part of me. But I had to learn to race from a place of joy. Not pain. Not sorrow. Not anger. Not to fix things I can't control. But for a connection with other people. With the wilderness. With myself. For the love of being alive, outside, and moving. Just joy.

It's an escape. Joe was right too. Racing is an escape from society. From symbols of status, from self-perceptions. A chance to just *be*. For everyone to just be, with each other.

When we emerge from the forest, we go for the final spear throw. I hoist a spear in the air and launch it at the target, but it falls short. Thirty burpees. Jimmy runs up along the fence to cheer me on. He's the only person out here in the dark, in the rain, besides a few waterlogged volunteers.

When I finish the burpees, I roll under barbed wire and

stare at the soapy wall. I couldn't do it the first time. I look around for someone who might be able to help, but there's no one behind me. Nobody coming. I walk to the side of the wall and start to do burpees.

The couple manning that obstacle look at me funny. "You don't have to do that," they say.

"But I'd feel kind of bad if I didn't."

"Please, just finish." I look up at them, standing there in their plastic ponchos. I do about fifteen burpees, then—

"Just finish!"

"Okay."

I get up and turn around to see a fire. Someone's been trying to keep it going, even in the rain. I don't think I can jump, but I hop over the flames and that's when I finally spot it. The finish line. The big black arch I could never picture in my mind but I see so clearly now. And standing in front of it is the final obstacle: a Spartan with a foam-padded pugil stick. The guy's supposed to whack me with it—give me one last Spartan jab. But he takes one look at me, puts his stick to his side, and waves me over.

"Give me a hug," he says. I start to cry. I've never cried at a race before. Tears trickle down my cheeks. I hope this stranger mistakes them for raindrops.

I hug the guy, then jog under the finish line in the quiet drizzle. There's no music. No announcer. No cheering crowd. Just a volunteer who puts a medal around my neck. I wipe the tears and water out of my eyes and look up to see Jimmy walking toward me, arms wide open.

Post Mudem

Roll Call

Of the 366 people who started the Ultra Beast, 161 crossed the finish line: 21 women, 140 men.

Just as he'd hoped, Cody Moat pulled away from Hobie Call after the log hop, running scared up the last climb, then sailing down the mountain at an unmatchable clip. He never looked back once to see where Hobie was. But when Cody came out of the forest, something happened that could have killed his lead in an instant: he missed the spear throw.

He feverishly tore through thirty burpees, finishing the last one just in time to watch Hobie's spear land in the grass. Victory was Cody's. He ran it in for the $5,000 win, then downed a Marathon Bar and headed straight into loop number two. He bested World's Toughest Mudder Junyong Pak by twenty-eight minutes for the Ultra Beast title, adding another $5,000 to his winnings. All in a good seven hours, one minute, and twenty-nine seconds of racing.

• • •

Hobie Call lost his title at that Vermont Beast, but he came back again determined to win. He stepped up the distance in his training and went for it. With NBC Universal Sports filming the event for a ninety-minute television special, Hobie won the race and the $15,000 first-place prize.

Irene Call hadn't run more than thirteen miles since her nine-year-old, Brooke, was born. Her goal was to place in the top ten in the Ultra Beast. After catching the same guy peeing in the same place on both loops, she pulled ahead of him and ran it in for a seventh-place finish, awash in a runner's high.

Like Hobie, Margaret Schlachter hurt herself before the Ultra Beast, rolling her ankle at another Spartan event. When OCR's first female pro rolled it again during the first lap of the race, she contemplated quitting. But she made up her mind to keep going, despite the pain and swelling. She grabbed her iPod Nano and tackled the second lap to the sounds of *Tron Legacy.* The movie's soundtrack played on repeat as she ran the trails and ski runs she'd grown up around. It was a final farewell to her home of the last sixteen years. After the race, she moved to Utah to live with her boyfriend, Hobie's brother, Forest Call. She was the fourth woman to cross the line, finishing in 9:44:24 — forty-four minutes out of the money.

After racing the first quarter-mile of the Ultra Beast on crutches, Todd Sedlak decided not to do any further damage to his broken leg. He chose instead to take one crutch-catapulted leap over the fire, then help other racers throughout the day, including OCR podcaster and future owner of the online magazine *Obstacle Racing Media* Matt B. Davis.

Matt knew he was going slow, but he didn't think he was

going *that* slow until he ran into a guy who had been lost for two hours. That guy decided to quit, saying he probably wouldn't make the cutoff after that disastrous detour, which made Matt think, *Am I that far behind?*

When Matt came into transition, he needed a break, and he needed real food. Todd bought him a burger, then Matt called his wife and chatted with her. All in all, he spent forty minutes in transition, thus breaking the number-one rule of ultraracing: just keep going. Eventually, Matt did keep going, making it all the way to the mile 10 gauntlet again. There he saw one of the race directors talking to another group of runners.

"I knew it was over," Matt says. His race ended there, but given the Spartan founders' reputation for playing mind games with people—telling them the Death Race was over when it wasn't just to see who would quit—I wonder what would've happened if Matt had ignored the RD and darted into the forest.

Daren de Heras and his teammates had only two miles left when they heard the horrible news: they were getting pulled. Time was up; they weren't allowed to finish.

Daren ran the Ultra Beast with Team SISU cofounder Matt Trinca and fellow Death Racer Mark Jones. The rules for team racing went like this: (1) Competitors must run in groups of three. (2) Each team member must complete every obstacle, no burpees, no exceptions. (3) Someone on the team must be carrying thirty pounds at all times—a log, a sandbag, whatever. De Heras's team picked a weight vest, and it made their lives hell. Dangling under the Tyrolean traverse with an extra thirty pounds strapped to the chest is no easy feat. Neither is making sure everyone on the team completes every obstacle. They knew they were going slow, but DNFing was never a concern.

"It was so difficult on all three of us," Daren says. Race officials put them on a bus with all of the other competitors who would not get that glow-in-the-dark medal. But the sad experience only made them hungry for more. "DNFing an event like that was the best thing that ever happened to me," Daren says. "It made me a lot more motivated. It fed the hunger."

Charles Maynarich became one of the 210 racers who DNFed. Did not finish. I never met him, but I'll never forget his turquoise bin.

World's Toughest Mudder Juliana Sproles chose to do the sandbag carry while her Mudder men and I did burpees instead. That choice put us ahead of her before we marched onto that never-ending uphill goat trail. We never saw her again on course, though she wasn't far behind; she crossed the finish line twenty minutes after me. "It taught me many lessons about tenacity and survival and enduring," Juliana says. "Even though when I finally crossed the finish line almost no one was in sight, this was definitely a highlight of my endurance racing experience."

Ray Upshaw spent a long time at the Tyrolean traverse getting pestered and harassed by fellow racers. Long enough, actually, that when he made it back around to transition, he was stopped. Pulled off of the course. There wasn't time, race officials said, for him to go back out on the second loop and make the required cutoffs. "It didn't break my heart," Ray says. He'd never been to Vermont anyway. The hills threw him off.

Months later he'd complete his fiftieth Tough Mudder and

take some time off from things. From hitting up every race, hiking all over the country, and sleeping under bridges. He needed time to reflect, train, and work on securing his NASM personal trainer certification because he wanted to help people in general, he said. That's what he was good at.

Eventually, Ray would be banned from all Tough Mudder events. The decision seemed somewhat unfair, given the free-for-life contract Ray signed with the company when he got his pledge tattoo. Tough Mudder accused Ray of selling the free-entry packets they'd given him to share with friends and claimed that action was grounds for revoking his lifetime entry. Ray is fighting the decision.

Robyn Dunn, my endurance partner-in-crime, recovered from all of her ailments and went on to qualify for the Boston Marathon at the Twin Cities Marathon. We finally competed together for the first time in more than three years at a Super Spartan Race in Temecula, California.

Jimmy became enamored with obstacle racing, particularly after he saw what the training was doing for his biceps. And particularly after he nailed the spear throw and went on to beat that guy he was racing in his wave. And particularly after he realized that the Ben & Jerry's factory is only one hour away from the Spartan World Championship.

Chris Davis, the guy who'd lost more than 100 pounds to attempt the Ultra Beast, began the race at four in the morning, flanked by Hobie's brother, Forest, two Death Racers, a disabled cop from New York, a Spartan employee, and Joe De Sena, who carried his 100-pound sandbag and was constantly tripping over things because he figured he didn't need a headlamp. Chris couldn't see the barbed wire he was rolling under, but he knew it was there.

His entourage slowly peeled off throughout the day until it was just him and Forest. Chris thought it was a challenge when a mustachioed racer brought him a bacon-and-egg sandwich. A practical joke. The delivery came as Chris was hiking along that goat trail, straight up the mountain after the mile 10 gauntlet.

Until he reached the log hop, he had his mind set on finishing the Ultra Beast. He would go until he could go no further. When he hurt his calf falling off of one of the logs, it suddenly became a struggle to finish just one lap of the grueling course, but Chris soldiered on to the end of the first lap.

He swelled with emotion after he crossed the finish line of the Beast, thirteen and a half hours after he set out on the course. He was a transformed man, his finisher's medal a symbol of months of struggle and the beginning of a new life, 123 pounds lighter than when he ran his first Spartan race.

It would be hard for him to leave Vermont and go back to life in Atlanta. "My friends in Vermont are extended family now," he said. "You don't go through an experience like that without making an extended family for life."

What happens next? For people like Juliana Sproles and Junyong Pak, Daren de Heras and Team SISU, Chris Davis, Ray Upshaw, Matt B. Davis, Todd Sedlak, Margaret Schlachter, and Hobie Call—people who have wholeheartedly adopted obstacle course racing as a way of life—that question is particularly poignant. Is OCR the first in a series of digital-era sports that catch on wildly, then fizzle just as fast? Or does it have staying power? Will OCR still be around in a few years?

Like all predictions, this one depends on whom you ask.

Some people will point to the struggles of smaller races as a sign that OCR has peaked already.

For example, Hero Rush, based in Columbia, Maryland, filed for Chapter 7 bankruptcy. *Men's Journal* had named the firefighter-themed 5Ks one of the "Best Obstacle Races," and Hero Rush had hosted fifteen successful events in the year prior to shutting down. But that wasn't enough to keep it going. Racers who had signed up for future events couldn't even get a registration refund; there was no money left. Hero Rush CEO David Iannone told his local news station that he wasn't getting enough participants to stay in business.

The Great American Mud Run suffered the same fate. And Superhero Scramble, a popular series that drew in elites with prize money, was scrambling to pay its winners after experiencing a downturn in registrations as well.

It's not just American series that are dying or struggling to get off the ground. Races in Australia, the second-most-popular country in the world for OCR after the United States, are suffering the same problems. "So-called entrepreneurs are becoming a little bit more aware that it's not as easy as it's made out to be," says Adam McDonald, chairman and founder of the Obstacle Course Racing Association of Australia, the world's first nonprofit dedicated to promoting the sport.

In fact, one of those American wantrepreneurs didn't even bother to secure venues or build obstacles. Racers who registered for the Critical Mud Run in Elizabeth City, North Carolina, lured by Groupons and a legit-looking website, showed up to the venue to find no race at all.

Perhaps the strangest of all the canceled-event tales comes from a series that asked Hobie to design its course.

With Hobie signed on, much to the chagrin of Joe De Sena, Extreme Nation jumped straight into marketing with

a military-badge-inspired logo and the tagline "Failure Is Not
an Option." The race would cover more than twenty obstacles
in two miles, and most important, the first event would mete
out over $100,000 in prize money. That got people talking. So
did the mystery surrounding OCR's newest benefactor.

"He's an ex-military man," said the director of operations,
Traci Martin. "He doesn't want fame. His goal isn't to be the
next Will Dean or Joe De Sena."

Obstacle racing blogs quickly pegged Richard Golden,
founder and CEO of the prescription glasses company SEE
Eyewear, as the man behind the event after finding a trademark document registered to Golden Challenges LLC of
Grosse Pointe Park, Michigan. They were wrong.

It was, in fact, Dr. Richard Golden, a Detroit dentist and
inventor of a tooth extraction device called the Physics For-
ceps. The man wasn't able to stay anonymous for long. Just
weeks after announcing the $100,000 prize purse, the com-
pany fired Traci Martin, writing on the race website that she
"strayed from the original vision for Extreme Nation and its
focus, venue and business plan." And in a totally unrelated incident, a week after letting Martin go, the body of Dr. Gold-
en's twenty-nine-year-old son, who had been missing for almost four months, was found in a landfill in a Detroit suburb.

That first race was indefinitely postponed. Almost as soon
as it began, it looked like Extreme Nation would disappear,
dashing the hopes of elite racers hungry for more opportunities to cash in on the sport.

With the "if you build it, they will come" mentality of the
early obstacle racing craze, too many events popped up with
too little to distinguish one from another. As a result, several
races have not had enough participants to stay profitable — or,

in the case of Critical Mud, have had no race at all. The little
guys, it seems, are cannibalizing each other.

But that doesn't necessarily herald the end of OCR. Some
futurists say the $1.7 million investment Dallas Mavericks
owner Mark Cuban made in obstacle racing company Rugged Races proves the sport is here to stay but will evolve as entrepreneurs entering the $250 million space shift the business
model. How? Hobie Call believes he has the answer.

After the Spartan Beast in Vermont, Hobie returned home
and got to work laying out his vision for the future of obstacle
racing. "Right now, the motto is 'longer is better,'" he wrote
on his website, Hobiecall.com. "The problem with this is that
people want this sport to require well-rounded fitness in order
to excel at it. But the longer races are for elite runners."

New races, Hobie decided, should be extremely short.
That would really level the playing field between runners and
CrossFitters, allowing athletes from all sorts of sports, both
endurance and strength-based, to become a part of OCR and
have a shot at winning.

Shorter courses would also be more fun for spectators to
watch and more TV-friendly. Airtime, Hobie believed, was essential for growing the sport. It would attract advertisers and
lead to better sponsorship opportunities for elite athletes, allowing guys like Hobie to race full-time more easily.*

It wasn't a far-fetched idea, or even a new one. Short

---

* Hobie's vision, incidentally, informed Extreme Nation's course design. The series ultimately did host an inaugural race, with a 1.5-mile course and a $40,000
prize purse. New tagline: "Extreme Prizes. Extreme Fun." The next day, however,
Extreme Nation fired Hobie and announced it would become a 5K event.

courses were already doing spectacularly well on American television. Modeled after Japanese shows, ABC's *Wipeout* and NBC's *American Ninja Warrior* had proved that modern audiences love obstacle courses. Done right, they make a fantastic spectator sport.

Wipeout first aired during the summer of 2008, billing itself as "the world's largest obstacle course." The show united everyone from children to grandparents by exploiting a simple truth: it's funny when people fall down. That's what one ABC executive told the *New York Times*. As the paper pointed out, it's particularly funny when people fall down in ridiculous ways, like bouncing over the show's trademark big balls or getting sucker-punched by a wall.

It's the same principle that made Electroshock Therapy a hit—falling contestants draw a huge audience.* Eight million people tuned in to *Wipeout* every week during the show's first few years on TV, and the National Association of Television Program Executives named it the third-most-popular game show in the world. (In comparison, during the 2012–2013 regular season, NBA games broadcast on ABC averaged about 4.7 million viewers.)

NBC's *American Ninja Warrior* took a different approach. Instead of putting everyday people through goofy tests of will and balance, *Ninja Warrior* built a course of back-to-back, upper-body-centric obstacles that only the strongest athletes could conquer. In fact, as of this writing, nobody has ever beaten the *American Ninja Warrior* course to claim the

---

* Like Electroshock Therapy, *Wipeout*'s obstacles also landed their creators in court. Tokyo Broadcasting System accused the show of ripping off several of TBS's game shows, including *Most Extreme Elimination Challenge* and *Takeshi's Castle*. Just as Tough Mudder and Tough Guy did, *Wipeout*'s creators and Tokyo Broadcasting System resolved the issue in a confidential settlement.

$500,000 grand prize. In its fifth season, the show was still go-
ing strong, attracting as many as 5.7 million viewers an epi-
sode.

Hobie wasn't the only person to take note of *American
Ninja Warrior*'s short-course success. So did a bakery in San
Antonio, Texas, that wanted to promote its new sports nutri-
tion bar, Nutridurance.

When a local mud run refused to let the Hill Country
Bakery hand out samples, its owners decided to create their
own event with back-to-back obstacles modeled after those
seen on TV. They enlisted the help of *American Ninja Warrior*
competitor Brent Steffensen to invent an amateur-friendly
Warrior course.

Calling their creation Alpha Warrior (tagline: "No Mud.
No Miles. No Mercy"), they set up 400,000 pounds of steel
in stadium parking lots in Texas and San Diego and lured elite
racers with a $3,500 prize purse.

But like many other races, Alpha Warrior quickly found
that trucking all of that equipment—five semitrucks filled
with steel, plus an entire semi stuffed with nothing but crash
pads—was a difficult and expensive undertaking. Add in per-
mitting, liability insurance, and site fees and the event production costs could crush their new company fast, as these
costs had done to so many others.

After hosting just two traveling races, Alpha Warrior
changed tack. The future of OCR, its creators decided, lay not
just in short courses but in dedicated OCR sites. The company started building Alpha Warrior Proving Grounds, workout facilities with both indoor and outdoor obstacle courses
where races are held outside while athletes train year-round
indoors.

Alpha Warrior now plans to build a total of twenty-five

Proving Grounds across the United States. "Setting up full-time OCR courses—that's where I see the real growth area in OCR," Adam McDonald says. "People will move away from trying to find a location and move more towards creating a really cool course that people can run every day of the week. Then they can start pitching that to commercial clients for team-building days. They can have clubs set up there, local racing, personal trainers can take their clients there for specialized OCR-type training."

Several people share that permanent-course vision. Before Alpha Warrior even started building its Proving Grounds, Rhino Course opened a similar facility in Las Vegas, offering unlimited use for $50 a month, as well as OCR classes and group training sessions. Three similar facilities, McDonald says, are already set up in Queensland, Australia.

These OCR gyms could survive on their own, hosting their own races and team-building events, but they're likely to draw more clients if they have something to train for—an event where participants get to face unfamiliar obstacles, new competition, rugged terrain, mud, water, and fire.

"You'll have these facilities that do the week-to-week-type stuff," McDonald predicts, though "you'll still need your big events," he adds. That means the OCR ecosystem depends on Spartan Race and Tough Mudder, two warring companies with radically different visions for the sport. One a millionaire's passion project; the other a young man's ticket to wealth and prestige.

From the beginning, Joe De Sena has said that he wants OCR to become an Olympic event. Getting to the Olympics, however, would require strict regulation of a sport defined by its unpredictability. The idea of imposing rules on OCR irks racers who treasure its rebellious reputation.

Triathlon, which was added to the Olympic program in 2000, faced the same issue in its early days, when it was also an unregulated sport that reveled in its renegade status. So far, Spartan Race has been following triathlon's path closely, making that Olympic goal less nuts—or hypocritical—than it may seem.

Consider this: Ironman was launched in 1978 with just fifteen competitors who were excited to face the unknown. Could they swim 2.4 miles, bike 112 miles, and run a marathon all in a row? When twelve of those athletes finished the race, the world had its answer. Yes, completing an Ironman is possible.

Just like the Ironmen who have gone before, all of the Facebooking, Twittering, GoPro-wearing Spartans have taken away much of the event's mystery. Ultimately, they've made it impossible to create an obstacle series in which nobody knows what to expect. Spartan's not going against any core principles by being open to regulation, one could argue; it's just evolving.*

Ironman's 1980 debut on ABC's *Wide World of Sports* turned the renegade endurance event into a captivating armchair sport. Spartan Race also made a television debut. Spartan's 2013 World Championship aired in a ninety-minute special on NBC Universal. The show attracted a similar number

---

* As Russell Cohen, Spartan's course build and logistics director, points out, standardizing OCR is a slightly more difficult undertaking than standardizing triathlon; for instance, it's hard to find several old tractor tires of the same exact size and weight.

of viewers as the network's yearly Ironman special, proving that OCR races can provide TV just as compelling as other established sports—and that there's a small-screen market for long OCR competitions.

The similarities between OCR and triathlon don't stop there. Two years after Ironman was first televised, a national sanctioning body for triathlon was formed. USA Triathlon's mission is "to grow and inspire the triathlon community." Among other services, USAT ranks triathletes across the nation with an algorithm designed to account for varying course lengths. USAT also provides liability insurance to races that pass its safety requirements.

In 2014 two entrepreneurs who shared De Sena's Olympic dream created OCR's first sanctioning program. While United States Obstacle Course Racing, which is modeled after USAT, has plans to offer ranking services, it's initially focusing on the liability insurance issue to help grow the sport. Insurance, USOCR's founders say, is one of the main costs prohibiting new races from entering the market. At one point, Will Dean said that Tough Mudder carried a $50 million general liability policy with Lloyd's of London. New races cannot afford a similar policy, though they could wind up facing similarly expensive claims. Pooling those races together under one large policy could drive costs down and help innovative, new races flourish.

Four months after USOCR formed, Spartan Race announced it would help create a nonprofit, international governing body called the International Obstacle Racing Federation (IORF), whose mission would be "to promote the sport of OCR throughout the world." It hopes to accomplish that by establishing safety standards, creating an international ranking system, and working with the International Olympic Committee and the World Anti-Doping Agency to make OCR an Olympic sport by 2020 or 2024.

Of course, it took another eighteen years after USAT was formed and eleven years after its international counterpart, the International Triathlon Union, started up for triathlon to make its Olympic debut. Right now, both USOCR and the IORF face an uphill battle in convincing events and racers that they're needed. But the striking similarities between the paths of the two sports thus far make it rash to write off the possibility of OCR evolving into an Olympic sport, as De Sena wishes.

For now, however, De Sena is focused on making Spartan Race profitable. It's a goal he hopes to reach in the company's fifth year of operation.

And then there's Tough Mudder. The event that's not a race. The business allegedly poached from England whose orange headbands became a defining symbol of the OCR craze. What is Tough Mudder's goal? What does Will Dean, OCR's slickest salesman, want for the sport?

It's tough to tell. I ran my first Tough Mudder with Jimmy a week after the Ultra Beast, and we had a blast. It was freeing not to worry about a race clock and to concentrate instead on enjoying our time with other Mudders outside in the warm Nevada sun. Even if Dean didn't invent the event, it took a flash of brilliance to see the need in the endurance sports market for an untimed, hard run like Tough Mudder.

Shortly after my Mudder debut, however, the news about Tough Mudder's legal spat with Tough Guy broke in an *Outside* magazine story, garnering national news coverage. Will Dean clammed up after that, speaking only to business rags and fellow Harvard grads about the corporate side of

OCR—marketing, brand recognition, and the like. He rarely if ever spoke about Tough Mudder as part of a greater sporting movement.

As a result, I can only guess what Dean sees in Tough Mudder's future. Perhaps he'll cash out when he's made enough money or profits drop, not interested in the future of the sport once he no longer has a business stake in it.

Perhaps Tough Mudder's ultimate goal, as Ray Upshaw put it, is to become the Subway of OCR. "They're not trying to be the best, they're trying to be the most known," Upshaw says. "Like you go to Subway for a sandwich because they're the most known," not because they make the world's greatest sub.

From a business standpoint, the Subway hypothesis makes sense: Tough Mudder has claimed to be profitable from the start. Why innovate or change when the formula is working?

Perhaps Tough Mudder cofounder Guy Livingstone best described Tough Mudder's ultimate objective in a *Fortune* magazine interview. "Our goal," Livingstone said, "is to become a household brand so that a guy can be at a bar and mention to a girl that he's running a Tough Mudder, and she can know what that is and be impressed."

Whether obstacle racing makes it to the Olympics or goes the way of distance plunging and roque,* there's no denying it's

---

* Actual Olympic events you've never heard of. Distance plunging, *Time* magazine writes, "required athletes to dive into the pool and coast underwater without moving their limbs. After 60 seconds had passed—or competitors had floated to the surface, whichever came first—referees measured the distance the athletes had drifted." Roque was similar to croquet. Just like distance plunging, it enjoyed a stint at the 1904 Olympics in St. Louis, never to return. Only Americans competed in both events.

had an indelible impact on participatory sports and America's view of fitness.

OCR ushered in a new wave of events that made running fun and accessible to millions of people who otherwise might never have entered a race—color runs, costume runs, zombie runs, midnight runs, dating runs.

OCR has given grown-ups permission to play, to explore, to get outdoors. To pick up rocks and logs and get dirty and run around with no fixed mileage or heart-rate goals. It's given us the ability to connect with other people on a pure and honest level, stripping us of any status markers and limiting self-perceptions and replacing them with mud. It's given us the chance to literally lend a helping hand, a knee to stand on, or a palm on the butt.

Before OCR, playgrounds were just for children. Now kids line up behind grown-ups to use the monkey bars and swings and ropes (at least on the weekends in Los Angeles). Training is no longer tied to distances run or biked or swum or skied. It's about being outside, enjoying nature, and making the most of one's surroundings. OCR has done more to make fitness fun for more people than any other sport in history.

Much more than a chest-banging, male-bravado-proving, modern-day tribal rite of passage, OCR is a powerful outlet for everyone from soldiers to bakers, bankers, lawyers, and even the homeless that helps heal mental wounds and strengthen bonds. It's given old athletes new hope, and new athletes passion.

Even after all of the drama with Tough Mudder, Ray Upshaw says he won't remove his pledge tattoo. Before OCR, he says, "I wasn't doing anything." But now, "I can honestly say I changed people's lives. I was a catalyst that caused change. To get rid of my tattoo is almost like getting rid of all of that. It's almost like none of that happened."

When I first decided to race OCR, it was with a heaping spoonful of skepticism. Some of my friends who would classify themselves as "elite athletes" pooh-poohed the sport for "making everyone an athlete" and celebrating mediocrity (criticisms mostly directed at Tough Mudder for not timing its participants and at all the many obstacle races that hold costume contests). But I was hoping to make a few new friends and lift myself out of a funk.

I did not expect that OCR would forever change the way I train. I did not expect that it would not only renew my zeal for sports but increase it. I did not expect to make so many sincere, motivated, and fun-loving friends.

Before I tried OCR, my workouts had become a mental battle that I no longer wanted to fight. I had cycling and running routes from which I would not waver—a routine that I had convinced myself had to be done completely, or not done at all.

Somehow, as I struggled through burnout, I stopped being active for the pure joy of it. I was just going through the motions of training out of forced habit. But OCR brought the joy back. It gave me permission to try new things and to "train" like I did when I was a kid and biked all over town for the hell of it.

Now I'll run without a watch, try new routes, and stop to swing across the monkey bars at playgrounds. I'll carry rocks and drop in the dust in the middle of a run to do push-ups. I'll race because it's fun to see friends on course, and because I enjoy the challenge, not always because I want to hit a time goal.

Of course, right when I crossed the Ultra Beast finish line, I wasn't thinking about how OCR would forever change me as an athlete. Or how the people I met on course would stay in my life long after we left Vermont. After the Spartan gladiator and Jimmy gave me a hug, I just wanted to take a shower.

SPARTAN ULTRA BEAST

2130-ish

After twelve hours, thirty-seven minutes, and fifty-two seconds of marching around Killington Ski Mountain, I stumbled straight into the hotel bathroom, where I stood in the shower in my muddy race clothes for half an hour. My hands were useless, puffed up like the Michelin Man's, and frozen. I couldn't bend over or grab my socks to pull them off.

Shivering under the hot spray, I thought about the race, a jumble of emotions swirling in my head. I felt elated. I also felt guilty that I put my body through that. Then I watched the thick, brown water trickle over my huge glow-in-the-dark finisher's medal and I felt proud.

As soon as I was done rinsing off, I'd have to update my Facebook status.

Extras

Mysteries Solved!

Mystery #1

On the trail, when I was trying to come up with a mantra to keep me going, I wondered where this came from: *You're stronger than you think you are, and you can do more than you think you can.* While I couldn't figure out where I'd heard this during the race, here are a few likely places I found afterwards:

Christopher Robin says something similar to Winnie the Pooh in the 1997 Disney movie *Pooh's Grand Adventure: The Search for Christopher Robin:* "You're braver than you believe, and stronger than you seem, and smarter than you think. But the most important thing is, even if we ever part, I'll always be with you."

Ken Chlouber, cofounder of the Leadville Trail 100 Mountain Bike Race, is known to give a speech before the race that incorporates the following: "You are stronger than you

think you are, and you can do more than you think you can!"
Jimmy participated in one of the qualifying races earlier in the
summer in which Ken made a speech that included this message.

Mystery #2

The water at the Trailside Inn tasted and looked like blood
owing to high amounts of iron in the local water supply.

Mystery #3

It seems improbable that Electroshock Therapy's wires are
juiced with 10,000 volts of electricity considering a standard
American 120-volt outlet can electrocute a person.* (Brief lesson in human-electricity contact lingo: *electrocuted* means
you're dead, while *shocked* means you're still alive.) We know
the obstacle has caused heart attacks, but it hasn't offed anybody yet.

So I contacted Dr. Michael S. Morse, a professor of electrical engineering at the University of San Diego, to see if the
10,000 volts claim could be true. Morse explains that while
10,000 volts can be life-threatening in certain circumstances,
it's possible for something to have 10,000 volts behind it and
be relatively harmless. "It might shoot off a large amount of
current for a tiny amount of time, but generally speaking, it
poses little to no risk," he says.

That's because many factors besides voltage are at play
in electric shocks. The most important of those variables are

---

* The answers here to mysteries #3 and #4 were adapted from my *Outside* magazine "Fitness Coach" column.

how much energy is driving the electric current, measured in amps (which is directly related to voltage), the frequency of that current, how long the shock lasts, and where it enters and exits the body.

"Household static shocks, for example, are very high frequency and have a very short duration," Morse says. According to LiveScience.com, it's possible to generate up to 25,000 volts by dragging your feet across a carpet, though Morse pegs the voltage of a typical carpet shock between a few hundred and a few thousand volts. Either way, household static shocks are almost always harmless. "Most of the shocks that electrocute people are at a much lower frequency, a much longer duration, and have more energy creating a much more significant driving force," Morse says.

Morse describes how humans experience shock in amps. Humans can feel one one-thousandth of an amp, or one milliamp, of electricity, he says. To put that in perspective, it takes about 800 milliamps to light a 100-watt lightbulb. Ten milliamps can cause a person pain, and at fourteen to fifteen milliamps, you will lose muscle control, an experience called the "cannot let go" phenomenon. Fifty milliamps is generally where you run the risk of dying from an abnormal heart rhythm.

Nevertheless, as stated earlier, how those amps are delivered plays a major role in whether or not you're toast. A Taser's current can exceed fourteen amps, and the devices can produce more than 14,000 volts across a human body. But their pulse lasts for only a few millionths of a second, and the average current they give off over time is less than four milliamps. (Researchers at Wake Forest University recently concluded that Tasers are generally nonlethal.)

"As a rule of thumb," Morse says, "amperage, in relation to

human contact, is about one one-thousandth of the voltage."
That would place Electroshock Therapy's amperage at about
ten amps, putting a shock from that obstacle on par with getting Tased. To make it worse, Mudders are usually wet when
running through the wires, and wet skin drops the body's resistance to electric shock.

In the end, whether or not you can withstand a 10,000-
volt Tough Mudder shock is a personal matter. As Morse
points out, "Humans are very variable, and some people are
vastly more sensitive to electricity." That's why Tough Mudder
makes it clear at the start of each event that if you have any
heart problems, pacemakers, or internal metal, or if you just
don't want to subject yourself to the shocks, you should skip
all electrified obstacles.

Mystery #4

My hands looked like I was wearing Minnie Mouse gloves at
the end of the Ultra Beast. They were bloated beyond recognition. I asked Dr. Bob Murray, the founder of Sports Science Insights LLC and the former director of the Gatorade
Sports Science Institute, what might have caused the issue.
Here's what I learned:

While eating excess salt in everyday life can cause bloating,
not having enough of it can cause swelling too. If you don't
take in enough salt while hiking but drink a lot of water, it's
possible to dilute the body's sodium to unsafe levels. When
that happens, you have hyponatremia. One of the symptoms
is puffy hands, because the extra water in your system enters
your cells and causes them to swell.

Should you OD on water and forget the salt, you'll probably experience other symptoms of hyponatremia as well, in-

cluding "headaches that won't go away, confusion that your friends recognize but you might not, irritability, swollen feet and ankles," says Murray.

How much water is too much? Everyone's needs are different. At rest, the average set of kidneys can handle up to a liter of liquid per hour, according to *Scientific American*. But while you're exercising that amount can fall drastically because your body releases an antidiuretic hormone that lowers the kidney's excretion capacity.

"If you get puffy hands, you don't want to disregard it," Murray says. "But nine times out of ten, it's just fluid pooling in the hands."

There was another, much simpler explanation for my Michelin Man hands: blood was pooling in them. If that was the case, Murray says, holding my hands over my head periodically, stopping to pick things up, and making fists to help move the blood back toward my heart would have helped depuff my fluffy fingers.

My Race Mantra

Endurance athletes of all types often prepare a few phrases to repeat during an event. The mantras may help them calm race nerves, be more competitive, or work through pain.

"I have positive key words that I say to myself," says World Champion Xterra triathlete Lesley Paterson. "I write on my forearm a certain word that triggers that emotion."

When she won her second world championship, BE BRAVE and I AM FREE were written on her forearms. A few others she's used: GRATEFUL and ATTACK. "I also use rhythms, like one-two-one-two-one-two, when the pain gets too much," Paterson says.

Hobie Call says he doesn't have a mantra per se, but focuses on his breathing. And when Junyong Pak is struggling for motivation, he says, "I tell myself that I have every opportunity to be as good as anyone in the world, and that determination is entirely up to me—the outcome something that I must live with." Not quite as pithy as BE BRAVE, but every bit as effective.

· · ·

Write your mantras here as you come up with them so you can pull out the right one when the time comes. Here are a few to get you started:

> Pain is weakness leaving the body.
> The faster you run, the faster you're done.
> Pain is temporary, quitting is forever.
> What doesn't kill you makes you stronger (best
>   if sung—in your head, for your fellow racers'
>   sake—to the Kelly Clarkson tune).
> When I'm done, I can eat an entire pizza.

Last-Chance Workout with Erik Taylor

Erik wanted me to leave home feeling strong but not too sore. Four days before the Ultra Beast, he took me through this final, full-body workout:

> Mummy walks (about 20)
> > *Swing a leg forward, touch your toes with the opposite hand, repeat.*
> Walking lunges (about 10)
> Foam roll
> Renegade rows (3 sets of 10 reps with 20-pound dumbbells)
> > *In plank position, holding on to dumbbells, do a row on one side, return to plank, repeat on the other side.*
> Circuit (five times through each of the following):

- 5 reps assisted chin-ups
- 20 lunges
- 16 wood chops (8 on each side)

We did these with Erik's cable pulley machine. Facing out from the machine, I pulled the cable from my right foot across my body and up above my left shoulder, then repeated on the other side.

- 15 V-ups

  Place feet in the TRX machine. Start in plank position, then raise hips up, like you're making a V-shape with your body. You can also do this with an exercise ball.

- 30 seconds battle ropes

  This takes two long, thick ropes. Hold one in each hand, then create waves with the ropes by squatting and standing while you raise your arms up and down.

- 1:30 rest

Stretch and roll

For more on Erik and training, go to www.eriktaylorsfitness .com.

Hobie's Post-Workout Wheatgrass Drink

Hobie swears by this wheatgrass drink to quickly heal sore muscles after a workout. Down one ASAP after a training session for a concentrated, anti-inflammatory dose of vitamins, minerals, phytonutrients, protein, and carbohydrates.*

Ingredients
2 to 3 Tbsp honey
2 to 3 Tbsp protein powder
    *Hobie likes Myozene Ultrapro (vanilla), but for the
    best taste he recommends Nytrowhey Ultra Elite
    (vanilla).*
1 serving of wheatgrass
    *Hobie recommends Pines wheatgrass powder
    (wheatgrass.com).*
1 tsp creatine monohydrate
16 to 24 oz. water

Shake it all together, and enjoy immediately.

———————

* Reprinted with permission from Hobiecall.com.